The Blue Room

Being the Absorbing Story of the
Development of Voice-to-Voice Communication
in BROAD LIGHT With Souls who have
Passed into THE GREAT BEYOND.

BY

CLIVE CHAPMAN (the Investigator)
AND His JOURNALIST FRIEND G. A. W.

First printed in 1928
Reprinted in 2017 by EML Media Group

CONTENTS

Chapter   Page

Foreword   3

I. The Investigator and the Medium   6

II. The Happy Band   11

III. Step by Step   28

IV. Rescue Work   61

V. A Typical Sitting or Circle   70

VI. Interviewing a Soul   80

VII. "Routine-keeping Intelligence"   91

VIII. Puzzling it Out   95

IX. In Conclusion   99

X. Some Explanations   104

XI. Testimonies of Sitters   116

XII. Professional Magicians Find No Flaw   136

XIII. Small, but Convincing Proofs   139

XIV. Extracts from Mr. Chapman's Diary   142

FOREWORD

THIS book is published with the object of disclosing to the world something new; something startling; something portentous. It is not, friend reader, "another of those Spiritualist books" with which the market has been flooded of late, books setting forth very much the same facts concerning experiences with orthodox mediums at seances in the dark. Before many pages of THE BLUE ROOM have been read it will have been realised that another and brighter beacon has been lighted for the benefit and guidance of the world, and even the sceptic will find in the extraordinary claims and happenings here recorded something that cannot fail to arouse his curiosity and his interest. For the revelation made in this book deals, mainly, with the phenomena of direct voice communication with "the other side" made in broad daylight and in bright artificial light through a medium and by means of sound vibration. Nothing like it has been successfully attempted anywhere in the world before: no other scientist, no other investigator, no other Spiritualist has obtained anything like the results which Mr. Clive Chapman has obtained. Word of this fresh phase of investigation and the success that has attended it has recently reached other countries, has been mentioned in Spiritualist publications in England, Australia, and elsewhere, and has already aroused the deepest interest in those essentially limited circles.

Has a new channel of communication been opened up? they ask. It has. Will this eventually lead to free intercourse with the souls of those dear ones who have gone over? to glorious revelations concerning the Life Beyond? and at last to materialisation and the joyous acceptance by the world of the assurance that indeed there is no death? Mr. Chapman hopes and believes that this will eventuate.

In this book is given the absorbing story of the development of this phase in the search for the Open Door; in it Mr. Chapman tells how he discovered the wonderful psychic power possessed by his niece; how he and she patiently experimented day after day, month after month, year after year, with slow, often halting, but always sure progress; how revelations came to him pointing the way, and how the happy band of souls on the other side who have been working with him have come nearer and nearer until now they are able to speak and sing with voices loud enough to be heard outside the closed door of the room in which the medium and the investigator sit. Thus it appears possible that the time is not so very far distant when this bright and glorious cable, so to speak, the construction of which has been a labour of love (neither Mr. Chapman nor his niece has ever benefited financially by their efforts here; on the contrary) on the part of the workers on each side, will come to the linking-up point. And then, What?

There is also set out here Mr. Chapman's experiments, and the results thereof, in phases other than that of the direct voice, results which have proved his niece (Miss Pearl Judd) to be an extraordinarily powerful all-round medium; detailed accounts of the sittings at which the messages have been received; short biographical sketches of the happy little band of workers now on the other side, and many other things which must be of intense interest not only to the student of the occult and to the scientist, but to every living person on this wonderful but tiny globe of ours.

I may add that when Mr. Chapman showed me his diary, his spirit drawings, his paintings, and the numerous other results of his remarkable experiences, I saw at once and made him realise that to let the world know how far he had gone in a branch of investigation never yet carried through to success elsewhere would be the means of bringing him a step nearer to the consummation of his life-long desire to bring light and comfort to his fellow creatures. As a journalist and something of a thinker, therefore, I feel that in collaborating with and assisting Mr. Chapman in compiling and publishing this book I am helping in a work that will prove not only interesting but of the utmost importance. I repeat, the book reveals something new; something startling; something portentous.

Doubters will arise, of course, and scoffers. They have already arisen here in New Zealand. Their arguments—fantastic, many of them—have been set forth in the daily papers throughout the Dominion. A number of them are dealt with in a chapter of this book. Mr. Chapman, by the way, hopes to follow the present volume with others dealing with the scientific aspect of his investigations, also the strictly spiritual and other aspects. Those who read the present volume thoroughly will realise the wonderful field for thought, discussion, and investigation this new phase opens up.

G.A.W.
Dunedin, New Zealand
November, 1927

CHAPTER I
The Investigator and the Medium

MR. CLIVE CHAPMAN AND MISS PEARL JUDD (G.A.W.)

Biography is, generally speaking, much more satisfactory than autobiography. Therefore I feel justified in taking it upon myself to write something concerning the history and methods of the Investigator (Mr. Clive Chapman), and the Medium (Miss Pearl Judd), the results of whose patient efforts form the subject of this book.

Until I met Mr. Chapman I had never given serious thought to any branch of Spiritualism, but a conversation with him so impressed me with his earnestness and purity of purpose, and so aroused my curiosity and interest, that I asked to be allowed to attend a sitting. This was shortly afterwards arranged and, one night at his humble home at 9 Quarry Street, Musselburgh, Dunedin, I had the privilege of being introduced to those Souls who had come to be so vividly and intensely a part of his life. This is one aspect of Mr. Chapman's genuineness that strikes forcibly those who are for any length of time in his company; his friends on "the other side" are so obviously real to him, and he is so quietly but firmly loyal to them; just as a strong character would be loyal to a pal or a friend for whom he had the deepest affection. Mr. Chapman goes even further than that; he has come to realise, after various demonstrations of their will-power and determination,

that, in the vital matter of developing the means of communi
cation, the lead must always be left in the hands of the higher
intellects on the other side. They are, I understand, at present
guiding him to greater accomplishments in the direction of
bringing the two worlds into closer touch, but they take their
own time, and never omit to check any over-eagerness which
he may—naturally enough in the circumstances—display.
"There is plenty of time" is their admonition, and it is on this
principle they work, smiling, doubtless, at the impatience of
the first-night sitter who demands to be brought into touch
with his own dear ones right away and to have disclosed to
him, or to her, there and then the great secrets for which scientists and others have been delving for generations. Mr.
Chapman is something of a scientist, though, without the
benefit of a higher education, he is largely self-taught. Patiently he has plodded along, using his naturally alert and critical brain, probing into the wonders of astronomy and of
physics, but above all ever strengthening the desire that has
possessed him since boyhood—the desire to do something
that will spiritually benefit his fellows.

And in this great work of linking up this world of ours with
the other side he sees his opportunity of silencing those hitherto relentless critics who hound down everybody who sug-
gests a future life, and those less bitter but contemptuous ones
who scoff at the idea that souls or spirits may hover round the
world upon which their mortal life had been spent; and in
compelling the orthodox churches to accept the fact that
there is nothing in the teaching of Christ that precludes a belief in direct communication with the so-called dead. Further,
this ardent seeker after truth is firmly convinced that, sooner

or later, scientific means will be found to make this communication easier, until some day it will be found possible for us mortals to mingle freely with our Heavenly visitors; and he goes steadily on investigating, always with the help of those beyond, to this end. A mighty work and a stupendous hope, you will say, and a work in which many have failed; though this fact does not deter him in the least.

And who, the reader will ask, is this man with such a mighty purpose and such wonderful faith. Where does he come from, and what is he like? Well, we have heard of great leaders— One in particular—who were of lowly birth and occupation. Mr. Chapman, the son of a tradesman, is himself a tradesman, a painter. He came out to New Zealand, with his parents, from England some forty years or more ago, when a very young child. He lived for fourteen years in the little coal-mining town of Kaitangata, in Otago; after which he came to Dunedin, where he has lived ever since. So that he is no stranger within the gates, so far as this part of New Zealand is concerned. Just a quiet living but friendly citizen, with no striking physical advantages to trust him upon public notice. He is, indeed, under average height, and slight of build, and his round rimmed glasses hide something of the eagerness of eyes which seem to be always watching for something to happen. He has an intense aversion to anything dishonest, anything "crooked," and his life and actions generally have proved that he practises what he preaches.

Mr. Chapman has had his troubles, domestic and financial, but is unmoved in his firm belief in the ultimate good.

How he became aware of the possession by his niece of such wonderful psychic powers is a story he tells for himself; I merely outline his personal history, because there are many who will say: "Who is Chapman, and who is Miss Judd? That is what you want to find out before accepting his story." And quite right, too.

So far as Miss Pearl Judd (the medium) is concerned, she is a Dunedin born girl, who attended school in this city, and has lived here all her life, which has been a simple one. Most of the time she has resided with her grandmother, her uncle also joining the household at a later period. She is just an ordinary happy young woman of nineteen, with all the healthy minded tastes and fancies associated with that period of a girl's life. She has no decided religious leanings, but possesses a strong sense of right and wrong and of justice. Though, naturally, interested in the great work in which she is engaged, she is not "vainly puffed up" because of her unique powers, to the development of which she has given much of her time. The nature of this work would, ordinarily, have often been such as to produce exhaustion, or at any rate intense weariness, but it is a curious and interesting fact that neither Miss Judd nor Mr. Chapman has ever felt the effects of strain. This, I take it, may be set down as a further proof that this particular phase of mediumship, or development of psychic power, is something entirely different to that already made known to the world. I may add in conclusion that it is to the credit of both Mr. Chapman and Miss Judd that neither has ever accepted any monetary return for their work, nor has any charge ever been made to sitters until quite recently when they set out on a tour involving a series of public demonstrations, for admission to which a nominal charge was made to defray expenses.

The Happy Band

THEIR HISTORIES

The contention that has been put forward in some quarters that the happy band of Souls who have come through so vividly to Mr. Chapman and others are mere mythical is disposed of by Mr. Chapman's ability to give something of the earth histories of most of those with whom he has constantly communicated. Many of them he had known personally in this life. Here follow these interesting histories, written by Mr. Chapman.

CAPTAIN TREVOR

Captain Trevor is one of the most interesting of our visitors, partly because of his deep interest in a particular phase of this work of ours apart from the voices. He came to us in January, 1927, and I recently discovered that it was from him that I have been getting a lot of my automatic drawings, especially those connected with the theory of production of sound waves. He is a great help in this work, and follows its progress very closely, giving the wonderful drawings just when they are needed. He has a very deep voice, and speaks in an abrupt, but distinct, manner, never wasting words, but just says what he wishes to say.

Often we hear his voice discussing matters with others "over there." He was an aviator on earth and went over as the result of a crash while flying as a member of the R.A.F. He plays the cornet beautifully, the tone being exquisite at times. He and Vilma often visit us together; they are evidently soul-mates, and a very happy pair.

RONALD

Ronald Travers is another member of our band. He came first to us in May, 1927. He, too, is greatly interested in the new phase, and he and Trevor evidently work together on it, for Ronald, like Trevor, was an aviator in the R.A.F. He came a crash at the Croydon aerodrome in 1924. In reality it was about that time we first heard of him, as he spelt out his name through the table, and said he would come again. We heard nothing more until he joined our little band in May last. He has a pleasant singing voice of tenor quality, and his speaking voice is easily heard.

GEORGE THURSTON

It was in March or April of 1927 that George Thurston first came through. He is evidently working with Trevor and Ronald in the new phase. He passed over during one of the Somme battles in 1916, and his brother, on attending our circle, quickly recognised his voice, and has had many quiet talks with him. George sings well in a light baritone voice, and, like all the rest of the band, revels in the work that has been allotted to him.

Charlie came to us about the beginning of February, 1924, and soon became popular with us and all the sitters. He is a strong, blunt personality, and he succeeded Torrance as "doorkeeper," a duty he has faithfully carried out ever since. He had been a soldier stationed in India, and went over while fighting against some tribesmen. By all accounts he put up a gallant fight against heavy odds, being all alone at the time, and fell covered with wounds. Such a courageous soul, therefore, is well fitted for the post of doorkeeper "over there."

On more than one occasion he has proved his strength of character by "carrying on" in the face of very bad conditions, when no one else could "get through" to us, and thus eventually overcoming all the obstacles and opening the door for a sitting after all. He is of the type, also, to keep away unruly influences from the circles, but for all that he has a pleasant sense of humour. His voice is of a strong tenor quality, and he sings splendidly. He helped a lot in rescue work among the darker spheres, work in which a strong, determined personality stood him in good stead. Large numbers of people have enjoyed Charlie's singing at the circles, and he is also ever ready to supply information concerning the life beyond. When he first came to us his sister was present at the circle; but she could not stand what she called the "uncanniness" of it, and went away. This hurt Charlie very much at the time, for even the strong souls "over there" preserve their sensitiveness. However, he soon recovered, and merely remarked that his sister "would learn someday." Charlie has been a staunch friend to me in many ways; helping me through many a hard fight. His personality never changes, and we all hope to have him with us for a long time yet.

GRACE

Grace was well known to me in earth life for about twenty years. She was, and is, a very spiritual and loving soul. She passed over at Wellington, N.Z., as the result of a severe operation. We had been great friends on earth, and she was not long in "coming through" to speak to me, first through the table, then by automatic writing, and finally by direct voice. The writing was exactly like her own, which the medium had never seen; and her voice, when she came and sang or spoke, I easily recognised. She and Dorothy knew each other well in earth life, and are probably helping one another a lot "over there." Grace rarely comes to us now, she having taken up work on the spiritual side further on.

OLIVE

Olive is my sister, who went over some thirty years ago, and who is also a rare visitor to us now. When she came my mother and I soon recognised her voice. She was a gentle soul, ever seeking to do something for the good of others, especially for little children or sick people.

JACK

Jack Sutherland came to us about the end of June, 1924, and I knew his voice at once by a peculiar catch in the throat which characterised his speech in earth life. No one else in our family had met him. Jack was a homely sort of man; big-hearted, but somewhat quiet in manner. This characteristic manifested itself when he "came through." He stayed with the band a long time, but is another of those who come only occasionally now, having been assigned other work. He usually sings in a quiet tenor voice, and likes to harmonise. He went to the war with my brother, and "passed over" in the first big Somme battle.

HORACE PRATTLEY

Horace Prattley came to us about the beginning of 1924, but it was some time before we knew who he was. He would often play a cornet in accompaniment to some of the songs played by me, and for many months we could not ascertain who this cornet player was. One evening Mrs. Prattley (a friend of ours here in Dunedin) came to a sitting, and when our cornetist on "the other side" spoke to her, she recognised the voice immediately as that of her late husband. He soon became popular with us. He was, and is, very fond of his two children, and converses with his wife about them at many of the sittings. His voice is of a pleasing tenor quality, but he loves to play the cornet, and does so as often as he can. This instrument he was very fond of playing when on earth, and continues to develop this musical gift. Horace was killed in France during the War. Joining up with this little band of souls he has remained with them ever since, helping on the good work with his cheery manner. He and Charlie have been great pals all through, and many a bright conversation between them we have listened to. This comradeship between these two souls over there is often expressed when they both come to a circle, and Horace talks to Mrs. Prattley; Charlie often chipping in, teasing both of them, Horace taking this in the very best of spirits.

JIMMY

It was about the middle of 1924 that Jimmy Hunter came to us, introducing himself to Pearl by automatic writing through her own hand. He told her quite a lot about himself, including the fact that he had been in the Navy. About a month after this Pearl was at a picture theatre when she heard someone mention the name of Jimmy Hunter, and all he had told her was discussed there in her hearing by two naval officers who were sitting nearby: I remember she came home that night very excited over the incident, which was to us yet another proof —if such was needed—of the reliability of the messages which came through. Jimmy is a very cheery and light-hearted soul; his voice is a high clear tenor and very pleasing. He loves to play the violin, and his playing is really beautiful, the tones of his instrument being of exquisite quality. There are times when we have wished we could see the instrument he plays, as under good conditions the tones are beyond expression in words. He has been with this band all the time we have been in contact with it; and has taken a great interest in Pearl, promising to teach her the violin, which he is apparently accomplishing. He was about nineteen or twenty years of age when he "went over."

JIM

Jim, who came to us towards the end of 1925, in September, I think, was very young when he went over many years ago. He has grown up in his spirit life, and his voice is now a deep rich bass, which is good to listen to when he sings. His mother, who attended some of our circles and had little knowledge of afterlife, was delighted and uplifted to know that her only boy still lived and could actually come and talk to her from that same "afterlife." His sister has derived great pleasure from many conversations with him, and it is very evident there is a strong bond of love between these two, which grows as the work continues. He remains with the band, and his singing of several good songs always gives great, pleasure to the sitters.

"GRANNY"

Granny was my mother's mother, and she has been over since 1911. She came to us in 1922, and comes at intervals to sing and talk, especially to mother. Her voice, a sweet soprano, is very clear at times, and is easily recognised by us all. The medium has never heard her sing in this life. Granny, when on earth, had a very generous nature, and would do anything she possibly could to bring cheer to other folk, especially children, of whom she was very fond. Often she had gathered a party of them around her, while on earth, and given them a right royal time. Granny's trials were many on this earth, but she faced them all, and is now very happy. She also has taken up the work further on.

HORACE BROCK

In February, 1924, Horace came through to us for the first time, and he has remained with the band ever since. A fine, straightforward personality, he is always welcome. He sings, at times, with Charlie. His brother Jack, on earth, has had several conversations with him. With Charlie, he likes to demonstrate how unlimited the power over yonder is by holding on to those long sustained notes in which Charlie so frequently astonishes the newcomers to the circle. Horace sings in rather a pleasing voice.

PETER

It was in rather a strange manner that Peter came to us. One Sunday morning, in June, 1925, I was playing the piano, and Pearl (the medium) was tidying up the fireplace when we both heard a tiny voice singing, apparently quite close to the end of the piano, as I played the hymn "Yes, Jesus Loves Me." The voice persisted, so I asked Pearl to sit in her usual place in the room so that we might see if the voice became louder. She did so, and sure enough the voice strenghtened, and I could the hear words. At the same time Pearl saw the singer clairvoyantly, and described him as a little fellow two or three years of age, with a head of golden curls, doing his utmost to appear manly. Peter has remained with the band ever since, and is loved by everybody because of his cheerful nature. He told us he was born in America, but of course, does not remember much of his earth life. He likes singing and talking to us, and at times is very clearly heard. At other times he appears to have difficulty in getting through; sometimes through conditions, at other times because of his gentle shyness. Lately, his great ambition has been to sing some of Charlie's songs, especially those with high notes in them. He also loves to talk about Jesus, and to try and help us by describing life as he sees it "over there." In the hymn "Yes, Jesus Loves Me" he always sings "Yes, Jesus loves Us.",'

HUNTER REYNOLDS

Hunter first came through about June, 1924, and he is still a member of the band. Possessing a rather light but pleasant voice, and a bright nature, he loves to sing at the circles with his mother, who is on this side. We have visited his parents' home many times, and he always comes to sing and talk, or to whistle. He frequently whistles the air of certain songs as they are played. He was a soldier and passed over during the Great War.

ANTHONY

Anthony Baum, who was a great friend of mother's, came to us at the beginning of 1925. His voice is of tenor quality, and he sings rather well. Mother quickly recognised his voice, although it is many years since she heard it on earth; Pearl never having heard it. Many times he has come to the sittings with Granddad, and loves to chat with mother, of whom he is very fond. He also comes very frequently with Hunter Reynolds, who is a great pal of his "over there," and remains an active member of the band.

VILMA

Vilma was unknown to us before coming through in March, 1927. She has remained with the band ever since, and loves to sing the more classical kind of music in a soprano voice of rare quality. It is glorious to listen to those high notes, which she takes so easily, often sustaining the top E flat without any difficulty. It is rather unique the way she plays with the melody, lifting her voice quickly from one note to an octave higher, and yet keeping strict time and tone. I have not yet found out when she went over, but Wee Betty has told us she was a Hungarian lady on this side.

WEE BETTY

The little soul who, always immediately wins the hearts of visitors to the circle, and who has charmed us and been loved by us ever since she came, in February, 1925, is Wee Betty. One evening we were holding a quiet sitting when suddenly we heard the voices of two children talking to each other. Both appeared to be taking good stock of us all, judging by their conversation. We ascertained later that these newcomers were Wee Betty and her sister Rosie. When we attempted to engage the former in conversation she proved to be very shy indeed, and had to be urged on by her sister, who seemed to enjoy the situation. Betty's shyness, it may be mentioned, is now a thing of the past, and her shrill childish treble constantly breaks in at the sittings, where she is, without doubt, "the life of the party." Rosie, by the way, she told us herself, had been run over and killed by a motor car, while Wee Betty informed us that her "Mummy" had jumped into the water with her in her arms. After questioning her further we came to the conclusion that she must have been drowned in a ship that was either torpedoed or wrecked some other way. The dear wee soul could not remember the name of the vessel; what impressed her most was the fact that her body lay at the bottom of the ocean and that she was free of it. She added that her mummy was all right, and was coming along to speak to us soon. This she eventually did, by the way, and we could all hear the joyous cry of Rosie as she ran to her mother's arms. The mother spoke to us very sweetly, and then the three chatted amongst themselves, evidently forgetting all about us for the time being. Rosie did not stay long with us, but went along with her mother, promising that she would come back some day and tell us of her experiences over there.

Wee Betty took some time to come out of her shell. A deeply sensitive little thing, we had to be extremely careful not to offend her by any hurtful remark. She gave out the whole of her little soul to cheer others, and if any of the sitters were gloomy it was immediately reflected in her. She, above all, best knows how to handle me when conditions during a sitting are difficult, and she is ever ready with some bright remark to ward off anything likely to upset me. She gives the impression that, if allowed, she would rush out and throw her arms around the sad ones and kiss and comfort them.
Betty has an exceedingly sharp intellect, is quick at repartee, and invariably too much for the ordinary mortal who tries to score off her. It is evident that this wee soul is put in the foreground to emphasise the true happiness and freedom which

exist over there; to show that one's earthly personality is re-tained at least for a period, and that the old idea of an entirely serious and saintly hereafter is wrong. "You don't think we just sit about on clouds and play harps all the time, do you?" asked Betty one night, and she added: "We've got lots of work to, do; but we never get tired."

Betty is a great companion of Peter's, and it is amusing to hear her mothering the lad. At other times she may be twit-ting members of the band, just as she does members of the circles down here, and her remarks are often quite frankly critical, though her nature is sweetness itself. Not always is she in "lighter vein," for she can discuss life and conditions "over there," and answer question after question put to her. Should something be asked about which she does not know, she will go off and seek the answer from some other soul, returning with the information if it is obtainable. She is a zealous mem-ber of the band, and expressively describes the work we are engaged in as "kicking a hole in the fence." "Love is every-thing" is her motto, and, according to her, they over yonder live on love; work for love, and strive constantly to bring love into the heart of everyone. Speaking to Betty is a refreshing experience, and one visualises a dear little mite of ten or there-abouts, intelligent beyond her years, with a keen sense of hu-mour, and a masterly, though motherly, and loving nature. I sincerely hope she stays with the band for a long time to come, for without her, many a sitting would be a compara-tively dull affair.

NELLIE

Nellie came to us on August 19th, 1926, soon after she "passed over," and has been a regular member of the band ever since. Of fine appearance and strong personality, she had been known to thousands of visitors to the New Zealand Exhibition held in Dunedin during 1925-1926 as the sweet singer of a number of ballads which were on sale there. Her early passing while in a strange land so far from home (which was England) aroused intense sympathy amongst the big-hearted Dunedin folk, and her last days here were marked by many kindnesses. One of the songs she had sung so many hundreds of times was "The Lonely Road," and it is when this is played that her voice comes through. The road is not lonely now, she tells us, and she is very happy. Nellie had had her troubles on this earth, but they have dropped from her now. Her voice is a rich soprano, and those Dunedin people who heard her sing at the Exhibition have no difficulty in at once recognising it. By reason of the fact that she was so well known here, her coming has convinced many sitters who were inclined to be sceptical.

DOROTHY

Dorothy was known to me for nearly twenty years in earth life, and was the first to communicate through this medium. This was about five years ago, almost immediately after she had passed over at Hastings, N.Z. She was thirteen years of age when I first knew her, and a very beautiful girl with the big motherly heart which still marks her character and personality. She was always wanting to do something for others, and she dearly loved little children. Dorothy has been a lovely control for the medium, watching over and caring for her in every way. On first coming through she proved herself to me in many different ways; stating her favourite colour; mentioning certain little incidents known only to the two of us; and helping me in my earthly battles just as she had so often done when here. Her voice is a strong contralto, and she now sings and talks in her old earthly tones, in which, however, there is a distinct spiritual quality. Her character has not altered either. Ever ready here to stand aside for others, she often now gives way to her comrades in the little band that they may have the pleasure of conversing and communicating with us. She has written countless beautiful messages to me through the medium by means of automatic writing, the text and signatures being very similar to her writing when in the flesh. The same sentiments run through these messages; love and concern for my welfare and for the welfare of all mankind. Time and again she has encouraged me with the assurance that the Silver Lining exists and will be revealed in God's good time. "Trust God and love one another" is the burden of her message, and I am content to do my best to carry out her wish.

Dorothy is the chief "Control," and arranges for all the sittings, and who are to be invited to them. For a long time after she first came through she helped us carry on rescue work for weaker souls (this phase of the work is described in another part of this book) and she is never happier than when she knows that harmony exists. A sweet soul, she has done much to bring this work of ours to the stage that it has now reached.

TORRANCE

Torrance is a very bright personality. He came through soon after Dorothy, to help her in the work, and proved himself in many ways. His parents live in Dunedin, and whenever we visited their home for sittings he brought through some excellent results. Torrance was killed in the Great War, and passed over while quite young. He had been very fond of his sister, and came often to the table to give us cheery messages. Several times he told us of a desire he had to bring through by means of psychic power coloured scenes of "the other side." Personally, I am quite convinced that this will some day be done. Torrance acted as "door-keeper" for some time, and was a pleasant soul to have near one. His voice has a fairly high pitch, and he sings the tenor parts of most songs beautifully. Finally he took up fresh work on the other side, and we hear him only occasionally now.

MARTHA MANSFIELD

Martha Mansfield came to us on February 28th, 1924, and has remained as one of the band ever since. She, too, is of a bright and cheery personality. She was a kinema actress on this side, and passed over as the result of being burned in a film fire. She explained to us that she had felt no pain. Her voice is a beautiful clear soprano of good strength, and it is most effective in solo singing, though she loves to harmonise at times with others. She has helped a great deal in the work, and her voice is clearly heard when she speaks to us and to the other sitters. Martha is of a sensitive nature, and prefers to come when conditions are at their brightest, being full of love and happiness. She at first referred on occasions to the pictures in which she had acted, but she does not now trouble about them, being happily engaged in work that is helping to prove to this world that there is a life beyond. Martha, was very fond of a joke sometimes, and had a trick of coming to the table to give a message to my mother when it was extremely inconvenient for the latter to answer immediately. I have not had an opportunity of seeing a specimen of Martha's earthly handwriting, but the messages we have got through from her are in writing totally different to that of Dorothy.

GRANDDAD

Granddad is my grandfather on my mother's side, and he often comes to us since his passing over, which occurred about three years ago. He used to help us in the work before he went over, and witnessed many things for himself. His going over was a wonderful experience for those who were gathered round his bedside at the time. He was fully conscious of the nearness of the end of his earthly life, and actually, in his last few minutes of consciousness, asked Dorothy to tell him by automatic writing through the medium what he must do as he went out. Dorothy's answer was "Do not worry at all; just let yourself go, and we will do all the rest. " Granddad appeared quite satisfied, and resigned himself to the end, as we mortals call it. It was a beautiful going out, and none of us felt sad about it; the other world seemed so close. We have often heard him sing since, at the sittings, in the same old voice he had on earth, and we also hear now and again the peculiar chuckle that he had made familiar to us. His was a very determined character on earth, and his familiarity with the Word of God as set out in the Bible helped him considerably to understand things about the world beyond, the Great Book being full of clear messages to those who understand and appreciate the importance of psychic power. Granddad still comes to us with the little band of workers, but not so frequently as most of the others.

SAHNAEI

Sahnaei is the Head Control of the band of workers who come to us. He first came through early in 1923. He was an Arab on earth, but has been over a very long time, probably hundreds of years, and he is in reality one of the teachers. He came fairly often at first while communication with the other side was being established, but now that matters are progressing steadily his visits to us are less frequent. However, if anything goes wrong he soon comes along and advises us what to do for the best, especially when the situation gets beyond Dorothy's powers of control. He is fairly strict, yet has a rather jovial personality; his deep sounding laugh being often heard, particularly when Wee Betty is up to some of her pranks. He is the guide who steers me through this work, and he constantly helps me mentally. By this method he reveals a lot to me, and makes it easy for me to explain the problems of life to people. He assisted Dorothy to come through when she made her first attempt to speak "on the sound," and many times he has helped conditions. His work, evidently, is to stand at the back of things, so to speak, and watch that all goes well. His singing voice is a deep bass, probably the deepest voice we hear, but he rarely sings more than one verse of a song. He has also spoken to us through a trance medium, and Pearl has seen him clairvoyantly.

CHAPTER III

Step by Step

MR. CHAPMAN'S STORY OF THE DEVELOPMENT OF PEARL'S MEDIUMSHIP

To state in a few words how I came to be in such close and direct communication with the life beyond would be impossible, so it becomes necessary for me to go right back into my young days and from there lead up to the point where I opened up communication through my niece's mediumship.

A VISION

The first incident which impressed me was a strange vision which I beheld when I was about eleven years old. I remember rising from bed one night and going through the house—it was in the country—on to a verandah, which ran across the back of the house. The night was clear and the sky full of stars, and I distinctly recollect feeling the chill of the night air as I stood there in my night attire.

Looking up into the sky I noticed that one star shone out more brilliantly than the rest, and, as I watched, a beam of light shot down from it and rested in the yard. In appearance this was like a searchlight, only not so bright. And, as I watched, a still brighter speck of light became visible on this beam, but far up in the sky, and appeared to be traveling downwards. Swiftly it approached, gradually assuming the shape of a draped figure, until at last it stood in the yard at the foot of the beam, a beautiful angel in brilliant robes; on its face an expression of infinite peace and power. The glow of the body shone through the robes and was so intense as to light up all objects for hundreds of yards around. I remember noticing at the time how several houses which stood some distance off, as well as the fences, trees, etc., were all made visible by the light or glow shining upon them, and that the ground and objects lying away from the light were in shadow.

I stood spellbound, watching. The angel did not speak, but raising its right arm, pointed upwards at the same time looking straight into my eyes and down into my very soul. Thus it stood pointing heavenward for fully two or three minutes, and all the time I felt a strange power surging from this glowing visitor all through me. Then suddenly, the figure receded up the beam of light, still pointing to the heavens, until it vanished from sight. The beam then faded, and darkness covered the land except for the twinkling stars far above; and I returned to my bed greatly wondering.

The angel was fully eight or nine feet high, and I can describe it as neither he nor she because the face and figure appeared to be both. There was such a beautiful blending of the two natures of man and woman in the expression of the face that it is beyond the power of words to paint. Love, strength, peace, power, mercy, humility, joy—all were here, and the impression it made upon me has never left me. Many times in the course of the last few years have I realised the purpose of this vision, if vision it was. In the light of subsequent events I am inclined to believe that I really did receive a visit from an angel in order that it might be impressed upon me the way I should take through this life, climbing that narrow way and helping others to find it. I am firmly of the belief that the same angel will visit me again in this life; when, I do not know, but whenever it may be I will be ready for more work for the benefit of my fellows.

STUDYING VIBRATION

Later in life I took up the study of sound and light, and their vibrations, especially sound waves, with a firm conviction that it would lead me on to the discovery of unknown powers which my very soul told me existed. Just before this I had come into direct communication with the outside world in rather a strange way. I happened to visit the house of some friends one night, and found three members of the family "having fun" (as they termed it) with a small table. They were sitting around it and getting messages—abominable messages—from some "spirit," which, immediately I entered the room, spelled out a very vulgar remark to me. I at once saw the danger, so I stepped in and stopped the "fun," explaining to those people that they must on no account encourage a spirit of that kind, but disregard it, and either do their best to bring a good one through or leave the whole thing alone.

I also urged upon them the necessity of treating the matter in a sacred manner. They had, of course, been quite ignorant of the danger of any harm coming from it, and I mention the incident so that it might be a warning to my readers never to fool, or play, with the powers beyond. Evil spirits are not difficult to call up, but the good ones have to be fought for.

From this on (about 1915) I came into touch with "the other side" in many ways; getting numerous encouraging proofs, even to the movements of the Allies during the War. Many of these moves were known to me before they took place, and it would have puzzled the British and French military leaders to know that I had these moves marked out on a large map often two or three weeks ahead. The revelations were perfectly safe with me, and I realise that they were given me to prove that a real intelligence was in touch, and to encourage me to continue the investigations which were opening the door into the Beyond.

So I determined to carry on, seizing every opportunity to communicate and studying every available book on the subject. I soon got better results, but also began to develop phases of mediumship (so called) myself. These came about unnoticed at first, but I was told to keep on trying. I had many disappointments, as well as many earthly troubles right in the thick of my first direct investigations. Then Dorothy, who has meant so much to me all through this work, visited us, and talked a great deal with me on the truth of communication. We neither of us realised how much those few short messages were going to mean to us in the near future. About sixteen months later she passed over to the life beyond, and almost immediately she came to me, first mentally, then through my niece by the table message, and giving me every necessary proof. She soon established herself, but stated that it was strange at first. Her coming encouraged me greatly, and I determined to face anything if it would enable those beyond to come further through the Veil.

DRAWINGS AND SKETCHES

Some time before this I had been getting a lot of automatic drawing through my own hand. These were of various kinds—statues, building, flowers,

figures, machinery, etc., and they convinced me that I was myself in direct communication with "the other side." I studied the drawings closely, and had a lot revealed to me concerning the conditions under which they were communicated. This phase has now developed to an advanced stage, and many intricate drawings of machinery, etc., have come through, but only when those beyond are willing; not just, when I want them. Many a time I have sat to see if I could get a drawing, but none came. At other times I have been able to get a great deal. The drawings are brought through in a strange manner, quite beyond my control. What I mean is, in quite a different way to that in which an earthly artist or designer would go about the work. No matter how anxious I may be to see a certain portion of the drawing finished, those in control continue on as they wish, guiding my hand in their own way and preventing it moving to any portion of the drawing but that upon which they desired me to work. If I persisted too much in my thought on my own desires in the matter, they simply suspended operations altogether; so that I have learned the wisdom of leaving it all to them.

I also discovered another phase of mediumship in myself; this was the ability to get coloured sketches of living persons' characters, in such a way as to reveal the whole make-up of their soul, so to speak.

Coloured crayons were used, the resultant coloured sketch indicating the particular person's virtues or vices. Thus blue indicated spiritual devotion; pale yellow, spiritual intellect; deeper yellow, pride; purple, spiritual power; pale rose pink, spiritual love; pale green, sympathy; dark green, jealousy; orange, earthly pride; pure white indicating purity. As these colours were blended or arranged together, so could I learn the spiritual characters of the persons concerned. The first two I got through

astonished me, and were so true (as I ascertained by enquiry) that for some years I refused to try for any more, being afraid of too startling revelations. However, a little while ago I felt I had to get character sketches of certain folk then visiting my home city, and these also turned out to be true to life. Once again, then, I had to face the fact that there was some power and personality from outside able to reveal, through me, what I could not possibly know otherwise about these people.

Then, again, for years I have been able to sit at the piano and play music I had never previously heard; sometimes playing for an hour or more at a time. It seems to flow in and I have to play it. This happens sometimes when I am alone, sometimes when others are present; but not always when I want to. In putting forward a few facts concerning these phases of "mediumship," or gifts, at the request of editors of Spiritualistic papers, I have been accused by non-believing critics of "blowing my own trumpet." Nothing is further from my desires; I just wish to show how the discovery and development of these gifts helped me to become more and more sensitive to the reality of the great outside world, and to fit me to go right ahead with the development of my niece's mediumship, which was opened up to me about this time.

There are all kinds of mediums, and all kinds of ways of using them. But they should never be used for the sake of material gain or for selfish ends; if they are so used, disaster is likely to follow. They should be protected from all persons who carry material influences about with them; for a medium is like a sponge and will soak in all vibrations as a sponge does water, and these are not so easily squeezed out. Once drawn into the world, a medium is difficult to work with; they should have the highest influences of a spiritual nature to help them on this side. The main thing is that a medium should be happy; no need for her, or him, to worry or study. Freedom from care in their case means the best result.

THE GREAT DISCOVERY

In the midst of a good deal of domestic trouble and mental strife in 1922 I chanced to visit my mother's home one evening when my niece (who was living with her then, as she is now) and others were present. In the course of conversation I asked them if they had ever witnessed any psychic phenomena. They confessed ignorance in the matter, and were, indeed, surprised to learn that I had been studying along those lines for years. It occurred to me then to experiment with each person present that evening (my mother, my grandfather, my sister, and my niece) with a view to finding out whether any of them possessed psychic power. They consented, and I arranged the alphabet in a certain way on the table and began. I will not explain the method I used, for being so simple, it is one that should be closely guarded, for reasons indicated in my reference to the two young girls to whom the bad spirit came through.

I tried each one in turn without result until I came to my niece, when the power manifested itself to a remarkable extent. Then, to my astonishment, the name "Dorothy" was spelt out. Then a rapid conversation followed. Dorothy urged me to keep on asking questions so that she could keep control and become stronger. She answered many of the questions I put to her, thus proving her identity; and at times she would ask me to wait until the power got stronger and she could speak more easily.

My readers may imagine the others' excitement and my own exaltation as the conversation proceeded. Dorothy referred to my troubles and encouraged me to face them out and to trust in God always, "as they did over there." They would help me through, she said. She also begged of me to guard and guide my niece (the newly discovered medium) in every possible way, so that the communications could develop along favourable lines. Evil influences must be excluded, for those souls "over there" wanted both of us for a great work. I at once realised what a wonderful psychic force was around my niece, and resolved to do my best to protect her, and to continue my investigations by trying out all phases of mediumship known to me.

For several weeks I visited my mother's home for the purpose of keeping in touch with Dorothy, and to develop the power, but held the sittings twice a week only. Next it occurred to me to see what could be got by the four of us sitting around a small oblong table with our hands placed on the surface in the usual way. The first time we tried we had sat for about half an hour when the dull sound was heard of knuckles or finger tips striking the under surface of the table top, first at one spot and then at another, and finally raps on the legs of the table. At my request, questions were answered by the spirit hand rapping out the letters of the alphabet, first on the legs of the table and then underneath the top. There was no mistaking the sound of a soft hand at work. After two or three sittings like this, all under electric light, other sounds came from the table such as those similar to wooden screws being turned, or a buzzing sound. The table would also move slightly.

VARIOUS PHASES DEVELOP

Now, this was all very encouraging to me; my niece had no knowledge whatever of psychic power or its meaning, and the others were impressed more by the uncanniness of the proceedings than by any other aspect. I continued the investigations further, and one night we were told to place our hands just under the edge of the table and wait. We did so, and slowly the table began to move, first one way, then another; it tilted over, then upended, and finally it rose from the floor, we keeping contact with our fingers meanwhile, until the top was on a level with our heads. Next it moved across the room until it rested on a larger table; then it took a tour of the room, turned upside down (in spite of our efforts to prevent it) and gave ample demonstration that some unseen power was controlling its movements. These demonstrations became much stronger at each sitting, and I asked one night if we might try the larger table. The answer was "Yes," and we proceeded to do so, with good results right away.

At this time my niece was getting clairvoyant also, which made a third phase to date. As we sat at the large table at meals, Dorothy would take advantage of the opportunity and spell out short messages, sometimes by taps under the table, at other times by slightly lifting the table at one corner and tapping out the messages with it on the floor. Much instruction was conveyed to me in this way, and it is astonishing what a lot of conversation may be got through when one becomes accustomed to the method. I became quite expert after a while and could generally tell what word was intended after two or three letters of it had been spelled : thus saving time. We had many interesting conversations by this means; all of us, including the medium, joining in.

Soon after this my niece developed the power of crystal reading. In fact she could see and describe scenes which formed before her eyes in any substance which was in the nature of a crystal. I was not in a position to buy the real thing, so I tried her with a large 5 in. condenser, which, being clear glass, answered much the same purpose.

Some of these scenes which she described to us were absorbingly interesting; many being events which had just happened, or were about to happen, in some part of the world. One night, for instance, she saw two aeroplanes approaching each other in a fog; they collided, burst into flames and fell. Next evening we read in our daily paper of such an event happening over the English Channel. Again she described a large building with trees in front of it. A man was seen to be hiding among these trees, and as a motor car drew up and a young man stepped from it, the one in hiding came forward and shot him down. My niece became very excited while telling us this, I remember, especially the shooting incident and the subsequent rush to the young man's assistance by others who appeared on the scene. Two days after this there appeared in the daily papers a cable describing just such a happening in Dublin, Ireland.

I could fill many pages in describing what my niece saw in these improvised crystals. There were great buildings, cities, trains, faces, interiors of rooms with people moving about in them. Often the scenes were of a celestial nature, and always they were in colour. Full details of them were conveyed to us by our medium, and I intensely regret not having written them all down at the time.

Some of the clairvoyant visions she described were also very beautiful; many of the people appearing in them were known to me and to others, but quite unknown to her. The medium took it all quite naturally and it was good to have it so, especially in a young child. The best results, I consider, are obtained with young people, so long as they remain unconscious of the full meaning and aim of it all. So soon as a medium becomes conscious of the great power surrounding her—or him—it often becomes spoiled by their misguided efforts to increase it. But so long as they leave it all to the investigator and do not bother to do more than sit willingly, good results will always follow. I have been assured that it is a most difficult thing to get a medium to see this point. When you have the privilege of investigating through one who does see it and acts upon it, then you have a Heaven-sent treasure that is well worth guarding and caring for. A human medium is an instrument, pure and simple, used by those beyond the so-called Veil to demonstrate unseen intelligence apart from the medium, and I would strongly advise all investigators—scientific or otherwise—to accept this fact. By so doing, and always allowing those on the "other side" to control conditions—no matter how good or how suspicious they may appear to be—convincing results will assuredly follow, if the investigator has the rare gift of plain sensible reasoning.

Very few scientists, alas, possess this gift: they demand a solid fact before they have given it a chance to build up, and never have the patience to wait when appearance seem to be against facts. This is where most investigators make a mistake. Scientists will never pierce the Veil by throwing bricks of doubt, scepticism, hard, material conditions, etc., at it. It must be approached as a loving mother would approach a child she adores, full of faith and trust. No other way will we get those beyond to come to us.

DEMATERIALISATION

Then there developed another phase; that of dematerialisation. Small articles such as lead-pencils, feathers, books, etc., would disappear to be afterwards discovered in all sorts of odd places. So I determined to develop this phase too. I possessed at the time a little red feather, about six inches long and very soft, and I used this many times in the experiments. Sometimes I would place it under a vase or a small box, and on looking for it a few minutes later find it gone. A hunt would reveal it in another room, perhaps. Once I asked my niece to place it in an envelope, which she sealed immediately, at my request. She then held it up to the light so that I could still see that the feather was inside the envelope, which she then handed to me; I opened it and found nothing. The feather had vanished in those few brief seconds, and on searching we found it in a vase on the mantelpiece in an adjoining room. Now, how did it get out of the envelope and into the other room unless it had been dematerialised and rematerialised? There were as witnesses of this occurrence, my mother, my sister, and a lady friend; all of whom were utterly astonished. At other times when the four of us were sitting at luncheon or tea, I would hide several coins under a piece of paper at the end of the table opposite and away from the medium. Before the meal was finished the coins would have disappeared. Occasionally two or three pennies would go; then, after a few minutes, one would be returned, then disappear again. On one occasion I said I would risk a ten shilling note. Bank notes of any description were not very plentiful with me, and I asked my spirit friends to be sure and return it. Dorothy spelled out through the table, "All right; just this once, but don't try it a second time or we mightn't let you have it back."

I folded up the note into about a one-and-a-half inch square and placed it under a book on the table and awaited developments. A little later I looked under the book. The note was still there. Would they be able to take it? We began to have doubts, but on looking a second time, sure enough it had disappeared. Then the table shook—their way of signifying laughter through the table—and there was no reply to my enquiry as to the note. We finished our meal and cleared away the dishes. Then, as my niece (the medium) stood just outside the door of the room, her back to the table, putting some dishes on the rack, I chanced to look on the table. And as I looked I saw a small and faintly misty something about half an inch square lying a foot away from the table edge. I could see the table cloth clearly through the object; which rapidly became more and more dense, or solid. I called out to the others to look also, and there before our eyes, tightly folded but opening out as paper so folded will do, was my ten shilling note. This was the only occasion upon which we have seen an object actually materialised before our eyes, but it was sufficient for me, as my faith is above phenomena seeking. I took it as just a little demonstration to help encourage me. I cannot help reiterating, whenever occasion arises, that to those who have real faith much will be given to strengthen that faith and to carry on the work of "opening the Door."

Once my mother put the little red feather under a heavy pile of books, and a few minutes later it had disappeared. On another occasion I locked up a sixpenny piece in a money-box, putting the key in my pocket. The first time I looked in the box I saw that the coin was still there but had been moved from one corner to the other. A second time I looked, and the coin had gone. Many instances such as these happened in our home, proving how strong was the psychic power that surrounded my niece, and how easily those from beyond could operate or communicate through this power, which is much the same substance as that of which their own world is composed.

Experiences such as those I have described must make one realise how completely we are in the hands of the powers beyond, and how helpless we would be if these powers were brought into full operation. To most folk all this doubtless appears uncanny; it does not appear so to me; it just convinces me of the existence of a world beyond this one, peopled by souls with power to help us in many ways if we will but meet them with faith and confidence.

Often as we sat at meals we heard a tapping noise on the floor or on the walls; sometimes quite near us; sometimes some distance away. The sound was as though someone was tapping lightly with a small stick. Again, would come the sound of a light foot-fall and a slight squeak of a boot; or rapid ticking would be heard. At times the table would tremble with a strong and very rapid vibration lasting for several minutes and causing my mother to grasp the milk jug to prevent the milk being spilt. One morning the vibration was as strong as that caused by a heavy motor vehicle when crossing the bridge. It stopped and re-started several times while at full strength.

LEVITATION

At this time we were allowed to invite a few people to witness these demonstrations with the big table, and on one occasion while six of us were standing around and holding it, it was suddenly elevated right above our heads, level with the electric light. As a test, I asked every one except the medium and one person at the other end, to let go their hold. They did so, and the table still remained suspended, the medium, almost on tip-toe while she kept contact with her fingers. Then I walked about underneath the table until it began slowly to descend to the floor, where it ultimately gently rested.

Following this, another person tried to lift the table again, but found it almost impossible to raise it from the floor. Further attempts were equally abortive until those beyond who were controlling the power suddenly switched it off, as it were, and the table could be lifted easily by an ordinary man's strength.

About this time, automatic writing had also developed through my niece, from Dorothy, and after several private sittings communication became very easy; writing being much quicker and more convenient than communicating by knocks. And these letters were wonderfully convincing to me, not only the messages and sentiments which they conveyed, but the form of the writing, which was scarcely any different to that of Dorothy's earthly writing. And remember, my niece had never seen Dorothy's writing. In any case, no person could forge hundreds of pages of another's writing without falling into errors. And the closest scrutiny did not reveal any discrepancies in these letters from my spirit friend.

It must be borne in mind that these souls who come to us do not lay themselves out to be always giving proof. They have the instinct of honourable persons, and you, my readers, who have similar instincts will surely understand the indignity of being repeatedly called upon to give fresh proof that statements which you have made, be they ever so new or startling, are not lies. I have had my proofs and require no more; yet these little messages of love and encouragement from Dorothy give me fresh strength to bear many worldly trials and disappointments.

Soon other souls from Beyond began to come through, and visitors whom we had invited to witness the phenomena were sorely puzzled at what they had seen and heard at our home. Next my niece developed the trance stage of mediumship, and soon my sister Olive and one called Torrance (the "door-keeper" at the time) as well as Dorothy, came through and spoke to us. During the development of this phase we had to use a dim light, and the medium went into trance quite easily, Dorothy having written previously to tell her not to fear, but just to let herself go and to leave the rest in their hands. It was a very sweet phase of trance, with no fuss at all, merely as though the medium had gone quietly off to sleep. And as the dear ones came through, they spoke very softly and kindly; encouraging us, and urging me to face everything for the sake of what would come later. Although the trance state developed so fully, those beyond have made very little use of it. They had greater revelations in view; their aim being to bring all they could through in bright light and with the medium fully conscious. This means that they come with their own power, through the psychic power of the medium.

OTHER DEVELOPMENTS

Subsequent developments have proved all this to me beyond a shadow of doubt; and many secrets have been revealed to me concerning the constitution of matter, psychic power, a medium's particular vibrations, the soul, the mind, and the body, until I see before me, startling as it may sound, the great possibility of communicating with our dear ones without the necessity of a human medium.

My investigations have led me in that direction, and I must continue on until the great secret is an open one, though only to those who can live so as to earn it, as it were. It will not be easily picked up, but will have to be keenly searched for, as Christ pointed out to us in all His teachings.

Having got this far I asked if we would ever hear them sing or speak direct, and was told "Yes, in about three months." So I made arrangements for the medium to sit with mother and myself.

I may mention here that often during demonstrations with the table or by automatic writing, Dorothy had asked me to play some music, hymns or otherwise. The reason for this will soon be apparent. It was evident that they were gradually leading the medium and myself up through the different phases of mediumship to that which they had been instructed to develop from their side with their own power, in combination with the psychic power round the medium, together with the utilisation of sound waves.

Knowing how keen and whole-hearted was my desire to solve the mysteries of life, these met me at all points and helped me to accomplish the object of breaking through the Veil. It has been glorious work, and worth all the trouble, all the battle, all the sneers. I consider myself very fortunate indeed to have had such a splendid psychic instrument as my niece placed in my care, and I had a firm conviction, when I opened up the direct investigations, that it was only by going through the stages of mediumship with her that I should get the higher forms of it eventually. Also I realised that I was dealing with intelligences who understood the conditions from their side far better than anyone, and it was my duty to carry out their wishes in every respect. Thus I was guarding against any hitch in the new development, a development which gave me so great an opportunity to discover and study many secrets concerning "the open door."

What better work could a man wish for? And yet, now that part of the results is being put before the public, it appears almost too much to take in. What will happen when the full results have been achieved and put forward?

After we had been told we would hear our dear ones sing and speak, we continued to hold little sittings, sometimes round the large table, which behaved in an altogether curious fashion. In addition to loud, rending, splitting noises, as though the table was going to pieces, there was the sound of rapping knuckles, and tap-tapping as with a pencil. Then the table would move about, until we would be forced to rise and allow ourselves to be pushed wherever those directing the movements desired. All this was a satisfying evidence of power. But there was still further evidence. I have seen my niece hold an ordinary metal tea-tray lightly in her hands while a big strong man grasped the opposite side and tried to prevent it being pulled from his grasp. At the end of twenty minutes strenuous work he had to give in, exhausted. My niece showed no signs of the struggle having affected her. Imagine a slim girl of fourteen years thus overcoming a strong man, and you will realise the amount of power put through by means of the psychic channel.

All these demonstrations, then, meant development and more complete control by those on the other side; and still fresh phases came along. Pencil sketches were the next proofs, a number of really, beautiful specimens coming through by automatic drawing, my niece's hand being controlled as in the automatic writing. Some of these were apparently symbolical; others were angelic faces with beautiful expression. Once a strange thing happened; my niece (who possessed no more than the ordinary school-child's ability with the drawing pencil) asked me to draw a barrel for her school-book on a piece of paper. I misunderstood her, and drew a wheelbarrow. She rebuked me, but as I had done the drawing on paper and not in her book I considered it mattered little, and proceeded to draw the barrel for her. The paper I was using lay on the outside cover of the drawing-book, and on my niece opening the book, imagine our surprise to find, several pages in, a dotted outline of the wheelbarrow—not the barrel—which I had drawn on a separate piece of paper.

There were six people present on this occasion, and they can vouch for the truth of my statements. But I asked for further proof, and, as a test, I drew a pyramid with a door at the side and a cross at the apex. Then the book was opened, and, right in the middle of the page this time, was an exact copy of my drawings.

THE DIRECT VOICE

It was shortly after this that we first got the voices. One evening I sat at the piano, playing "He Shall Feed His Flock," while my niece was doing her school home-lessons, and mother reading by the fireside. The latter suddenly looked up and said she was sure she heard a woman's voice singing, seemingly far away. I continued playing while the three of us listened intently. At first we could hear nothing; then all at once, near the end of the verse, there came faintly a female voice of exquisite quality. I thought it might be the echoes of the piano deceiving us, but, as though in answer to my thought, the voice stopped, then started again, and sustained several of the notes. It was all very faint yet; but each of us heard it, and my joy may be imagined, for I realised in a flash what it all meant. My way was made clear, and I made arrangements to go ahead with this latest phase.

The first evening we sat by the light of one candle only; my niece at one end of the piano; my mother at the other; I at the keyboard. I played each piece of music over and over again; often ten or a dozen times, before the voice was heard; then it would come in just near the end. I came to the conclusion that the reason for their wanting me to play an air many times over was that the tone peculiar to that song might become, as it were, leveled down to the vibrations suitable to the soul singing it, and to which they could tune in. This revealed to me a really beautiful science, and made me more determined than ever to put all my available time and energy into this development.

After a few sittings the female voice became clearer, and the man's voice was added, though the latter was yet faint, as the former had been at the outset. I asked Dorothy to tell me, through the automatic writing, whether I should try a horn for the purpose of concentrating and intensifying the sound of the voices. She replied in the affirmative, so I utilised the phonograph horn which we had in the house. Placing this on top of the piano with the wide end facing myself and the other end so placed that my niece could rest her hands upon it as she sat near the piano, I played "Onward Christian Soldiers," several times over. For a while we got nothing, but I persisted. Then came a woman's voice of contralto quality, and it was so exactly Dorothy's voice that it actually startled me for the moment. I knew her voice on earth so well that I could not be mistaken. She sang two or three songs and hymns several times till I could hear the words quite distinctly, especially the line "marching as to war." She then stopped, but on my playing another tune she again sang to my accompaniment. Then a man's voice said, in a loud whisper, "Father," and the sitting ended abruptly.

Now, I consider these results marvelous for a first attempt. Much more startling phenomena have, I know, been recorded as taking place at dark seances, but with all due respect to those human mediums who were responsible for bringing these about, I must say, here and now, that I have reached the stage when I can accept nothing as absolutely and finally conclusive unless it has taken place in full light. It has been laid down that darkness is essential to manifestations, but I have disproved this. Our little band of souls from Beyond have told me time and again since those early days of experimenting, that darkness is not only unnecessary, but that they do not like it.

It must be borne in mind that, at these earlier sittings, the conditions were of the best. There was my own unshakable faith that the thing could be done; there was the strong psychic power round my niece, coupled with her entire lack of knowledge of psychic matters; there was my mother, a patient and loving sitter; the sound waves of harmonious music; and, above all, there was Dorothy's intense desire to get through. All this made for good results, and I am often thankful to God that these first attempts were so successful, for we later experienced, owing to mixed conditions, many disappointments.

We received instructions soon after this to be very careful who we invited out to our circles, as those "on the other side" were particular as to who the medium came in contact with; they did not wish to waste power combating detrimental influences. This supervision was a pretty difficult task at times, but I had to face it for the sake of protecting my niece's mediumship, which was now rapidly developing to an advanced stage in this latest phase of direct voice communication. At each sitting, still by candle-light, the singing got louder and more distinct. One night I stopped playing so that I might hear the full power of the voice come out through the horn. The voice sang on for a little while, and then faded slowly out, and, though I resumed playing, we got no more. Afterwards Dorothy wrote through my niece saying that I was never to do that again. It appears that the sudden stoppage broke the power they were using to come through and nullified their efforts. They depended upon me, said Dorothy, to keep the sound going continuously. After that I was always very careful never to stop until they told me to, and I also made a point of keeping the right pedal down all the time, so as to have a continuous flow of sound.

I had discovered that the voices came best on a steady flowing tone, and that the ordinary way of accompanying did not serve the purpose. At first the louder I played the louder came the voices, the power and clarity of which always astonished the newcomers to the circle.

Another big step forward came when those from "the other side" refused to use the horn any longer, and we sat and listened for the voices coming in "on the sound" or "on the air," so to speak. They became more and more strict as to details; the songs to be used, the order in which the sitters were to take their places, and so on. The positions we now occupied were : my mother by the fireside, my niece seated at a large table on the opposite side of the room, and I at the piano; each of us being about nine feet apart, thus practically forming a triangle, and these positions were kept at every circle held in our house for the ensuing two years. This uniformity of method is always an essential condition in psychic experiments and development, a fact that few scientists or investigators fully realise. By this means, however, and by combining my knowledge with the knowledge of those Beyond, all the time giving way to their wishes and directions, I arrived, after encountering and eventually surmounting many, many obstacles, at a stage which had placed me in the position to pursue and study the development of a still more advanced phase of psychic power. What this is I shall not here disclose, though I hope to have advanced sufficiently far in it to give it to the world at no distant date.

Progress became rapid, and we were allowed to bring a number of people from time to time to hear the singing and to witness other demonstrations. When there were no sittings my niece read or did her school-lessons, while my mother usually read and I very often played the piano. We had long ago placed our coming and goings, our method of living, and our lives generally, in the hands of those on "the other side." And it may be seen that, while arranging the conditions so that our daily lives would be inconvenienced as little as possible, they made them such that they were favourable to the voices coming through almost at any time and in the full light. On many nights, as my niece was busy with her home-lessons and I strumming at the piano; one or another of those happy souls from beyond would come and sing. Some of the voices were of exceptionally sweet quality, and often two could be heard harmonising.

INSTRUMENTAL MUSIC TOO

And they did not stop at vocal music. Soon the sound of different instruments were heard; the violin, the cornet, the 'cello. There were other sounds, too, the nature of which we could not determine. Songs which these dear souls consider the most suitable for producing the particular harmony they desired were asked for by means of automatic writing, and, if we did not have copies of these, they asked, "Would you mind getting them for next time?" At this stage each voice came on a particular song, and if it happened to be inconvenient for a soul to come through, I was not allowed, try as I might, to play her or his song. I found that these songs had the same effect as calls, and naturally, a soul would not wish to be called if engaged in work elsewhere, any more than we on this side would like to be disturbed at our own appointed tasks.

It also became evident to me that these souls were acting under strict orders, and had certain phases of the work under their care, in connection with the new development. Many of our friends who visited the circle were unable to understand why those on "the other side" were so strict, why they did not just act as they (the sitters) wished. I had to frequently enlighten them on this point, and even then I could see they were rarely satisfied.

And so the voices continued to come; the medium might be washing the dishes or cleaning the range, or sweeping, and I playing the piano, when we would hear one or other of our soul friends singing. Not so distinctly as when we all sat in our proper places in the circle, but yet clearly enough to distinguish the voices. We began, too, to distinguish the words of the songs, those dear ones helping us in this direction by singing certain lines over and over again until we did hear the words. Again we discovered that there was method in everything they did. This training of our hearing, so to speak, was for a purpose, for not long afterwards the sweet singers began singing messages to us, replacing the original words of the song with the words of their messages. The power of conversation not having developed yet, this was made a step in that direction.

Thus, step by step, not "all at once," as most newcomers wanted it, were we being brought together, and just as surely will we go on developing until, in God's good time, the door will open wide. To my knowledge, the method I am employing and the lines upon which I am pursuing my investigations, have never been practised by any investigator in the world before. It is not an easy method, and more than mere scientific knowledge is required. I plod on, having faith and praying for patience and loving sympathy; all of which are essential to gaining the assistance of the workers "on the other side."

I was told by Dorothy to try and find eight or ten psychic persons as nearly as possible with the same quality of power as that surrounding the medium. As it may be imagined, this has proved a very difficult matter; so much so that up to now I have discovered but two. Now and again I come across a likely subject, only to find on scrutiny that there is something or other in them which makes them fall short of the necessary standard. I am convinced that, so soon as I am able to gather together the right ones who will be prepared to put everything aside to help me open the doors, wonderful results will come; happenings such as the world has never seen, but which Christ told us about many centuries ago.

Now began to come to us several new souls; some giving their names through the table; others through the automatic writing, and others again by means of song. It was at this stage that Charlie came to us through the table, and it was not long before we heard him singing to us at a sitting. From the very first it was obvious he thoroughly enjoyed the experience, just as we on this side enjoyed it.

The power had developed to such an extent now that we were given permission to visit a friend's house and hold a sitting there once a week. At first it took a little time for those Beyond to become used to the new conditions in another home; but the piano there was a good one, which helped considerably, as the music produced had a better and smoother harmony than was possible from my instrument, a comparatively small one.

At this particular home we obtained, later on, some rather strange results. On one evening everyone but the medium and I were told to proceed to different parts of the house and listen. They went, and returned with wonderful stories. Each had heard a different instrument being played; one a cornet; another a flute; another a violin; still another a 'cello, and so on, six or seven distinctly different sounds in all. I, at the piano in the room, heard the voices. The piece I played was "Home, Sweet Home," and the harmonising of the spirit voices was glorious. At other sittings in this house we heard sounds as though stiff brown paper was being rustled; and twice some of us heard a loud rushing sound overhead. Again, there was the sound of running footsteps across the floor, also of dancing feet, the vibrations being plainly felt.

In our own home the power continued to grow stronger. Two or more voices were now heard singing together, as well as the accompanying instruments. Some of these instruments we could not place, even experienced musicians failing to recognise them. A remarkable thing was that the medium herself rarely heard any of the voices, unless they spoke direct to her. Another proof that those dear souls were really there was given when I played some entirely new music (inspirationally) and one or another of them would sing it note for note exactly as I played it.

Then there was the scent of flowers. Oftentimes when certain souls were near us we could discern the scent of certain flowers in the room. If it was Dorothy who came it would be a strong scent of roses, a flower she loved. Or if Martha Mansfield was with us it would be the scent of violets. Others brought lavender, or narcissi, or musk. Once, when an Arab came, there was that unmistakable stuffy odour that clings to the wrappings of an Egyptian mummy. Three times I have noticed the scent of roses while I have been playing the piano at a sitting, or while writing; and once or twice when I have been at work. But when it comes in the presence of my niece it is always stronger than when she is not there. And these scents come whether the flowers are in season or not.

I now took to recording the rapid developments of the various phases of psychic power; and a busy time I had of it. As the voices gained in strength, the sittings became more frequent and the hitherto strictly enforced conditions regarding the positions, etc., at these sittings were relaxed by our soul friends.

There was no longer need to sit in absolute silence without moving. Objection, however, was taken to any talking going on while a song was being sung. Some of the sitters, becoming excited, would chatter; thinking that, because the singers were invisible it did not matter.

It was not long after this—about June, 1924, that I was informed that attempts were to be made to speak and converse, as well as to sing. What a thrill went through us as we watched and listened for this wonderful development. I was told to play a piece called "Yoo Hoo," evidently because of the particular tone it produced. I noticed, as a matter of fact, that after playing the piece over several times a kind of set tone, or vibration, was set up which was continuous. And it was on this wave that we first heard our soul friends speak to us. Just a word at a time for a start. Then a pause, and a song as though to gain power for another attempt. It is always towards the end of a song, by the way, that the voices are at their loudest, hence the using of this method to get in the precious word.

Our excitement and our eagerness may well be imagined. We had reached the long-sought phase of direct communication in full light. We were on the verge of conversing in these surroundings with our dear soul friends. Who was to know to what it would lead! After a few sittings we could easily hear them speaking whole sentences and conversation at last became an accomplished fact, conversation between us and our friends on "the other side," and by a method never before attempted in this world.

What possibilities it opened up for me from a scientific stand-point, and what comfort it was to bring to thousands on earth thus to be convinced—for surely it is impossible, in the circumstances, not to be convinced—that there is indeed a life beyond. As these souls came through and spoke to us, greeting us with cheery words and unmistakable delight, their joy and satisfaction at having got through to speak to us was unbounded. To us, too, it was wonderful, too wonderful to be fully realised; and in the passage of time it becomes more wonderful still.

After all these years to have succeeded! After all these years for those patient, loving ones on the other side to have got through by a method which allows them to come under their own power, added to psychic power of a medium!

Let me state right here that my niece is, in the ordinary sense of the term, not a medium. The power is around her for the present, for certain reasons, and is well guarded, both on "the other side," and on this. All the money or all the kingdoms in this world would not tempt me to divulge the secret of it to anyone; it is too sacred to play with.

I made it my life work to study it out; I prayed for it and strove for it, and God graciously revealed the key of it to me, through my niece. Besides hearing our dear ones speak directly to us, we hear them oft-times conversing among themselves; often, too, they laugh. This, doubtless, will be a shock to those who think of "Heaven" as only a solemn place; but it is indeed good to hear the dear souls so cheerfully happy.

At this stage we were carrying on a "rescue circle" every Sunday evening to help those souls on the lower spheres to advance. I have described the wonderful happenings at these circles elsewhere in this book.

CHAPTER IV

Rescue Work

The simple, direct language in which Mr. Chapman tells of
the Rescue Work circles gives a sufficiently vivid picture of
that striking phase of life beyond. Here again is the old absurd
idea of an idle, aimless, harp-playing existence dissipated.
Those who have come in contact with the great-hearted
Samaritans in our big cities : men and women who sacrifice
worldly ambition and comfort that they may bring a little
happiness to the less fortunate in this world, will the more
readily understand. Who, having been present at a Rescue
Work sitting, could have the effrontery to put it all down to
fraud or trickery; to ventriloquism, or wireless, or dictaphone?

"One of the most interesting phases of life on 'the other side,'
" writes Mr. Chapman, "is the Rescue Work carried on in the
denser spheres by those in the brighter spheres, especially by
those on the plane with which we are in touch. It is rather difficult to convey in words to the reader a picture of this great
work, but I will do my best, and I only hope that serious
thinking people the world over will soon realise how necessary
it is for those on this side to learn all they can about life beyond before they 'go over,' and so make the task of those engaged in rescue work on the other side so much the easier. As
it is, the lower or denser spheres must be tending towards
congestion, and those on these spheres, being unable, in spite
of the help given them, to rise rapidly, are becoming a menace
to the minds of all on the earth plane.

"I hope the reader sees what I am trying to convey, and recognises the necessity for serious thought concerning life generally, but especially in regard to life 'over there,' where we will, without doubt, 'reap what we have sown.' Just think of the millions upon millions who have gone over in ignorance or doubt; the cruel, murderous, envious, jealous, mean, covetous, proud, selfish, lustful, and many others: can you wonder at those other bright and happy souls being eager to break through the Veil and to try and make this world understand the reality of life beyond, so that no more need go over in ignorance and sin to those darkened spheres?

"Another important thing to remember is that most of those minds in the denser spheres are actively, very actively, at work influencing the weaker minds here on earth; so that it is incumbent upon those of us who are awake to the powers of mind and their everlasting connection with the eternal soul, to help here, just as those dear souls are helping over yonder, to bring light to those darkened souls by rescue work. We can do our share by fighting hard to get people to reason out for themselves the great difference between body and soul; that the body is but a machine controlled by the soul while here to carry out its earthly requirements, but absolutely useless when the soul leaves it, and that the soul does live on after leaving the body, is indeed more full of life than ever. Certainly the body has to be cared for, but not lived for, so that at so called 'death' we may move right on and not be held back by any strong earthly desires that will drag like an anchor.

"Now, as to those Rescue Work Circles. This work requires the very best of conditions, so that, generally speaking, only my niece, my mother, and I sat, but occasionally a friend would be asked to help. These circles were carried out in quite a different manner to the ordinary ones, and every care was taken on both sides to bring about the most harmonious conditions so that nothing would hinder the task of bringing into the circle any soul that needed help. It was no easy task, either, to get some of them in. We would often hear either Charlie or Dorothy, or perhaps Torrance or Martha, persuading some stubborn soul to come.

"You see, the idea was, mostly, to bring in souls who had gone over in ignorance of the fact that they were free of earthly conditions and of the body, and to get them to see, while they were with us, that this was so. It was remarkable how these poor stubborn souls would put up all sorts of arguments, too; probably just as they had been used to doing when on earth. All sorts of personalities were brought in, and we could distinctly hear the conversation between them and these dear friends of ours who were trying to help them.

"One of these, I remember, was a soldier who must have been badly smashed up at the war, and was still under the impression that he lay in a pool of blood. For a long time he could not be convinced that there was no blood there, and—judging by his remarks—insisted upon showing his hands to Charlie, who, in turn, was doing his best, by dipping his hands into the supposed pool and showing them to be clean, to convince the distressed soldier to the contrary.

The aim was to get the soldier's mind away from the scene of bloodshed and from the thought that he was still in his mangled body. He must have passed over in awful agony, for his groans and cries were just as much as we could bear. All this is another proof of the power of mind, for although this poor soul was right away from his torn body he thought he was still in it. And it was, apparently, a difficult matter to get his mind off that thought, and here is where the beauty of the work of those bright rescuing souls comes in. As I played the piano and Dorothy sang, the groans of the soldier soul gradually ceased, and it was obvious that he listened and watched, for, after the third verse of the song had been sung, he asked 'who the shining lady was.' We told him it was Dorothy, and spoke a little to him. He still thought a bit about his leg being off, but Charlie's proofs had evidently had an effect and aroused joyous doubts in his mind. He could be imagined moving about, for expressions of wonder and of pleasure came through to us, and after thanking us all, the rescued soul went away with Charlie, singing and happy. Tens of thousands of such souls are over there, doubtless, all being held back from the brightness awaiting them because of their ignorance of the life beyond, or their refusal to believe in it.

"No wicked or desperate souls were brought into these rescue circles; the conditions they would have brought with them would be too much for us, and break the circle. As it was, Charlie had on two or three occasions to be very firm with some of the poor souls brought in, their language being distinctly of the earth earthy, and coarse at that. One, I remember, swore so profusely that he had to be returned whence he came, and as he went off, jeering at Charlie, the latter remarked that the poor chap would be given another chance at some other time.

"Horace often played the cornet at these circles, and many a soul forgot his troubles while listening to this celestial music; some even wanting to try the instrument themselves. Several who were brought into the circle possessed good voices, and after they had been brought to realise where they were, they would treat us to a song. One, named Arthur (I forget his surname), had a magnificent voice, and it was indeed a treat to listen to him sing a message of his own to us to the air Cantiqua de Noel, by Adam. His voice was very similar to that of Caruso, and the high notes were simply wonderful. The effect was that of a voice sounding away down a long corridor, but clear as a bell.

"Some who came were really funny, and were obviously amused at us sitting around talking to them; others were as blunt as could be, while others again were gloomy or sad. One dear old lady would not go until she had told us in detail all about the garden she used to tend on earth, and how she loved to take big bunches of flowers to sick people and to the hospitals. This old soul would go away, but return immediately to tell us something else. This she did several times, and we could visualise those dear rescuers standing by patiently, smiling. Charlie told us afterwards that it helped souls like that old lady's wonderfully to chat a bit with us. Many who came asked for some favourite hymn, and to hear Dorothy or Martha singing it with them was good indeed.

"Those whose condition was too bad for them to be brought into the circle had to be helped in their own sphere, and this work appeared to be attended with a certain amount of risk, the very best of conditions being essential before our dear ones would allow us to hold an open circle while they went into those denser spheres. Several times a rescue circle was suddenly closed because of disturbances beyond our conditions : the controls would take no risks; they were considering us.

"Wee Betty, after her first introduction to us, often came to talk while the rescue work was going on, telling us excitedly how matters were progressing, though at times she seemed just a little afraid, especially should one or other of the band appear to be in difficulties. This penetration into the denser spheres must naturally have been something in the nature of a Great Adventure to those of the band engaged in the work. Difficulties are sure to be encountered, and danger, just as they are by any expedition penetrating into the wilds of Africa or South America, where more or less unknown conditions exist.

In the rescue work 'over there' their strong love for one another and their firm faith in God is the greatest protection these bright souls have against all dangers. Several times one or another has penetrated too far and has, in a manner of speaking, been 'lost' for a short time by being cut off by those in this sinister sphere. This is observed by the other rescuers, and things get busy. There is a great stir, and I am told to play a hymn softly and to continue to play it. Then, all at once, seemingly from afar off, is heard the sound of the 'Machines:' They approach rapidly with a rushing noise, go by at a terrific speed, and recede out of earshot just as rapidly. Wee Betty became very excited the first time she saw them, and when we asked her what they were like, answered 'Like big silvery fish going at lightning speed.' Five went by the first time we heard them, and we were told that the machines were under the control of those higher up, who were in charge of all rescue work. Our informants added that whenever danger threatened a worker one or more machines were immediately rushed to the scene of danger and checked it by the use of their power to rescue the rescuers, so to speak. If the invisible power we have had demonstrated to us through the table is a small sample of what can be applied when necessity arises, it can be readily understood what tremendous forces those beyond, in their rapid vibrations, have at their command. No sphere with a lower vibration could withstand such power.

"Doubtless all this will appear as a fairy tale to most readers of our book, but we who have been privileged to hear the rush of those 'machines,' and the description of the work by those on the scene, have no hesitation in accepting it all as absolute fact. The experience is unforgettable, as is the sensation which came over us at the thought of the appalling power possessed by those beyond. And those of you who will read your Bible properly will find frequent references to these powers as used through all the ages, but always well guarded, as they are now. Just think : if a nation procured control of a fraction of such a power and used it for selfish purposes—as no doubt it would—or worse! But no earthly nation or people will be allowed to obtain control, and if ever the power does come through to us it will be for the purpose of bringing universal peace. Yet, strangely enough, the power itself is around us in abundance; is right here with us, but the one and only key to it is held by Him who holds the earth in the hollow of His hand.

"Several times during our rescue sittings these machines were brought into action, and one night when Charlie got into difficulties and was cut off, no fewer than sixteen went by, some at tremendous speed, others not so fast. That night Wee Betty was given a treat in the form of a ride in one of the machines as it returned. Her delight knew no bounds, and as they started away we could hear her calling 'Good-Bye.' One very faint comparison to the whole scene would be the turning out of the world's strongest fire brigade to a disastrous conflagration in a very big city. The Chief Control (Sahnaei) once told us that those machines on the other side travel as fast as our light does. We could not look upon them, as a matter of fact, unless we wore a mask to protect our eyes, and even then they would look just like flashes of intense light to us.

"The singing at the rescue circles was always very beautiful; mostly hymns or harmonised songs. Occasionally a soul would ask for a song he or she had once known, but which I did not know; in this case we had to compromise. I could not count the number of souls brought through these circles, or the scores of voices—men, women, and sometimes children's—that we heard. It was all very instructive, too; Betty, Peter, Charlie, Dorothy, Martha, Horace, or Jim often telling us of life on the other side in all its phases. Being at the piano all the time I have not, much to my regret, been able to take full notes of the conversations. At ordinary sittings others have done this, and a summary of many of these are given in another part of this book.

"To my mind, the greatest lesson to be derived from these rescue circles was the realisation of the fact that these bright and happy souls left their own beautiful sphere to enter darker and, as we have seen, dangerous spheres in order that others less fortunate than themselves might be helped to realise that there is a brighter and happier life awaiting all those who will but try to attain it by putting their trust in God and loving one another. Indeed, that is the watchword over there, as it should be on earth; 'Trust in God and Love One Another.' "

CHAPTER V

A Typical Sitting or Circle
(G.A.W.)

To the investigator and the medium, familiar down the years
with the procedure, the surroundings, and the result, a "sitting" is but part of their daily lives. At this stage they see
nothing new in it; and for them, the time when they mar-
veled and wondered has passed.

Therefore it is perhaps better that a mind upon which all this
has made but a recent impression should convey that impression to the world while it is fresh, leaving the explanation to
the mind that has become matured by long experience, study,
and knowledge of the truth of the revelations.

I will take my readers with me to the outlying district of
Tahuna in a suburb of St. Kilda, Dunedin, and to a small
house lying under the shadow of a beetling cliff out of which
stone is quarried for metalling the streets. Indeed, the street in
which the house is situated is called Quarry Street, and it is
one of those partly-formed thoroughfares upon which the
pathways are more or less swallowed up in long grass, and
where properly channeled gutters are not to be found. Entering, I am welcomed by Mr. Chapman, and by his mother and
his niece, and introduced to other visitors who had arrived before me. Among these are a theological student, a corporation
official, a lady and gentleman from Australia (the latter a
prominent official in one of the big cities of the

Commonwealth), a musician well known to vaudeville pa-
trons, and others. After chatting together for a while, Mr.
Chapman asked his niece to ascertain (by automatic writing)
if "they" would be willing to give a demonstration with the
table for the benefit of the newcomers. The answer was in the
affirmative, so eight of us gathered round the oblong table,
which was about 8 feet by 3 feet, placing our fingers under
the rim of the table-top and lifting the table until the legs
were a couple of inches or so off the floor. Three of us were at
one side, three at the other, while Pearl (the medium) was at
one end and Mr. Chapman at the other. A minute, perhaps,
elapsed, then Mr. Chapman remarked "Come along Charlie,
or Trevor," and then things began to happen.

Gradually the weight of the table doubled-trebled-quadru-
pled, until the strongest among the men were obviously being
tested to their utmost to keep it from the floor. The sinews of
their wrists were seen to be straining, while their faces wore a
grim look of determination to "hold on." Suddenly this exces-
sive weight was removed from some but not from others. My
neighbour on my right gave a sigh of relief, "Thank goodness,
it's gone." Another at the far-away corner at the opposite side
said: "I've lost it too." But it remained with me, and with
most of the others. Then a lady remarked "That's funny; I feel
the weight in one hand and not in the other." A similar experience befell a gentleman at the other side. Then we changed
places to see if we would be treated the same as those whose
places we had taken had been treated. Some were not. It was
evident that the unseen were directing a power just as one of
us might have an electric torch where wherever the beam fell a
leaden weight became apparent.

After this the table swayed and turned round, pushing us hither and thither, and sometimes shaking up and down, as if conveying the laughter of the unseen humorists who were having such a game with us. Next we felt the weight altogether leaving our fingers, and the table rose steadily till it stopped just clear of the electric light globe, some seven feet from the floor. We kept contact with it, but our fingers merely rested under the rim; there was no weight. Then, with a swaying motion akin to an aeroplane, the table swooped down and I expected to hear it crash to the floor, but it eased up, in a manner that could not have been managed by any human beings bent on trickery, and settled gently on its castors. "That was Trevor," said Mr. Chapman, "he was an Air-force officer you know."

Remarkable as this demonstration was, it was not sufficient to convince me of the existence of spirits. I had heard so much about table turning and how it could be done by human agency, that I decided to await further developments before expressing any opinion, though I had no reason at all to doubt the honesty of Mr. Chapman or his niece. At any rate there were no Houdinis among those present on this occasion.

We next adjourned to what has come to be known as "THE BLUE ROOM." This was a smallish room about fourteen feet square, papered and curtained in pale blue (the spiritual colour) and with a pale blue silk shade over the three electric light globes, which were, I guessed, each of at least 50 candle power. The only object on the walls was a framed lithographed copy of the famous picture "The Light of the World," and this hung over the fireplace, in which a bright fire burned. The only furniture in the room was a piano, two very small tables, and a chair for each of the sitters. Nothing else. And all the while the three 50 candle-power lights were burning brightly; at no time during the sitting were they switched off.

A heap of songs was handed to me, as being the first sitter in the circle, and I was asked to choose one in readiness for the commencement of the "concert." In the meantime Mr. Chapman seated himself at the piano, and began playing a composition of his own, which he calls "Roses I Bring You." He had played the air perhaps three or four times over, when a mezzo-soprano voice, faint but distinct, was heard apparently just above the medium, and humming the tune in unison with the piano. Then another voice, a man's this time, joined in. This was beginning to be interesting; but the sounds were faint, and it was difficult to do what Mr. Chapman had told us newcomers to do, namely, to "take no notice of the piano, but listen to the voices." The piano, which was admittedly not one of the best, would obtrude upon our aural nerves; at least for a while. Afterwards we did manage to ignore it to a certain extent.

I may explain that the sitters were arranged in a semi-circle, with the piano at one end of it, and a little detached, while the medium sat behind one of the small tables, in full view of us all from start to finish; sometimes smiling at one or other of us; sometimes swaying the leg she had crossed over her other knee; sometimes tapping with her fingers or making other such movements as any fairly high-strung person would do while sitting apart and saying nothing for three hours at a stretch. It must be remembered (this I was told after the sitting) that the medium hears little or nothing of the voices from beyond unless one of remark souls is addressed exclusively to her by one of the souls.

The voices became stronger after some five minutes or so; and (I have particularly noted the possession of what we would call "good manners" by the members of the little band) always addressed themselves to the strangers first.

"Good evening, Mr. _ ," said a voice, addressing the gentleman from Australia.

"That's Charlie," remarked Mr. Chapman, and the Australian visitor, obviously puzzled, answered "Good evening, Charlie."

"Pleased to see you here tonight," Charlie proceeded, and an appropriate answer being given, he then paid his respects to each one in the circle.

"Hello' everybody," piped a shrill child voice, and all except the first-nighters eagerly replied, "Hullo Betty." For it was "Wee Betty," the bright little soul who had been and was to be the tiny "sparklet" who kept the proceedings moving merrily along. For indeed "a merry, merry soul was she." Betty hullo 'd us all, addressing me as "Uncle George," and the vaudeville artist as "Uncle Gregory."

"So you've got a night off at last, Uncle George," said she, alluding to the fact that owing to my newspaper work, I had been unable prior to this to fit in a date for a sitting.

A little more light chatter, and then I handed in the song I had chosen. It was "The Lonely Road," and as I passed it over to Mr. Chapman, Betty chuckled. "Ah, ha!" she said, "Uncle George wants Nellie," and immediately there were calls for "Nel-lie," and whistles, as though the person called was away down a lengthy roadway, or across a wide paddock. Now, it will be noted that I had not mentioned the name of the song nor had the pianist begun playing it, yet the young sprite Betty had divined my wish. The song recalled to us incidents connected with the death of a young singer of personality who had sung this same song many hundreds of times at the New Zealand Exhibition. I had become acquainted with her, and, later, during her final illness, had joined with a few others in providing little attentions which made the last days of this stranger in a strange land as comfortable as possible. Nellie "came through" all right, and sang the song; I immediately recognised her voice, which I had heard sing the same words many scores of times on earth. It was a strange experience now to hear it sung in what we orthodox mortals are wont to call "heaven," or rather, by a heavenly visitor. It was still more thrilling for me when on a later occasion Nellie sang a song the words of which I had written myself. This song had been published after her death, and it was noticeable that, as she sang it, she slurred or hummed over some of the words, just as a mortal would do who had but imperfectly learned them.

Well, after the singing ceased I, on a signal from Mr. Chapman, said, "Hullo! Nellie."

"Hullo! George," she answered; "isn't it lovely to meet again?"

"Do you remember the old Exhibition days?" I asked, and the voice replied, "Rather; but I wouldn't be back there again for anything." I referred to letters I had received from her people in England, and she remarked "That was very nice." I expressed my intention of writing again and telling them of this meeting, and she said "Yes, do; they would be so glad to know I am so happy. You may tell them," she added, "that it isn't a lonely road any longer.'

I was at a loss as to how to proceed with this strange conversation, and there was a pause. Presently I heard Nellie's voice talking and being answered by Charlie. It was clearly an "aside" as it were, and I heard her mention my surname twice. It was clear that she was explaining to Charlie her earth acquaintance with me. I mention all this to show the naturalness of the proceedings, and the impossibility of any "faking."

The next song chosen was "Take a Pair of Sparkling Eyes," and we were told that we were in for a treat, as this was one of Charlie's favourites. And Charlie did indeed sing it beautifully. That last note, which is such a telling one with all tenors, was taken with a ringing clarity that was, in the circumstances, startling, and on its repetition I counted twenty-four beats as the length of time this celestial vocalist sustained that last note. I was told that this was nothing extraordinary for Charlie, who had been known to sustain it for minutes without "taking breath."

Charlie, after his song, was engaged in conversation by several of us, and cheerfully answered all questions put to him. Asked by the student as to whether those who "went over" continued to grow older, he said that the young ones did, but that the older ones grew younger, so that eventually they all reached what would be the ideal age on earth, say about thirty. Other questions were asked and answered.

A characteristic squeak by Wee Bettie sounded as though it were right in our midst. "Where are you, Betty?" asked a lady. "Here in the room, of course," she answered. "Can you see us?" urged the questioner, and Betty replied, " Why, of course I can."

Just at that moment one of the sitters placed his thumb to his mouth, and Wee Betty immediately shot out, "Are you hungry, Doc?" Another sitter was feeling in his upper vest pocket, for his watch, and again the little voice came : "Don't put your hand over your heart; you're not Napoleon." This, I take it, was to prove to us that she could indeed see us all.

Dorothy's sweet voice was next heard; her song being "Beautiful Garden of Roses." Her singing voice was a very beautiful one, and her speaking voice equally so. She conversed with Mr. Chapman freely, and he declared to us that he discerned the scent of roses. The others did not get it, but I did on another occasion, though not on this.

Songs from Jim ("Shipmates o' Mine"), and Martha ("Love's Old Sweet Song"), and a little chat with each, and then the vaudeville artist, who was a particularly fine violin player, played the "Indian Song." He had got half way through it when another violin joined in. It was Jimmy playing a duet with the earthly violinist. That it was no echo was proved by the fact that Jimmy, purposely maybe, was frequently half a beat behind or in front of the other player, and the tone of his instrument was different. All the voices acclaimed this new sitter who came to them with such music, and wanted more. He next played Mendelssohn's "On Wings of Song," and when he had finished, Charlie, Betty, Dorothy, Jimmy—all of them, thanked him and said they "Could not get enough of that." "Uncle Greg" had indeed "made good" with the folk "on the other side."

Next little Peter responded to "When Autumn Leaves are Falling," his boyish soprano struggling with the song, and being helped along by the others. One could imagine these bigger and older souls standing by ready to help the younger ones if they got into difficulties with their singing or in their conversation. Wee Betty was put forward as a mouthpiece, because, I was told, hers was the voice most distinctly heard, and, further, she had mastered the art of "getting through," and so had plenty of confidence. Her repartee, bright "chippy" talk, and cleverness generally were really wonderful. On one occasion she parodied a song really well, her words being comments on something that happened during the sitting. Had this brilliant little soul grown up on earth she would, I should say, have been a very clever woman.

And so this sitting went on; song and conversation alternating. Nothing very deep or illuminating was revealed to us on this occasion, but this was explained by the fact of so many newcomers being present. Invariably, when new sitters are there the conversation and information is on an elementary plane, so to speak. So Mr. Chapman informed us. But to we newcomers, it was all very wonderful; very puzzling, and the remark I had once heard concerning animal performances came to my mind "It is not so much that they walk on their hind legs so clumsily; but that they should walk that way at all." And I thought, "It is not that the conversation was of such an ordinary character, so much as the fact that we were able to converse with them at all!"

All the time, as I have said, the medium was sitting in the full light. I watched her throat and mouth and chest carefully (her dress was the usual low cut dress worn by girls) and failed to see any movement of any of them. This, then, disposed of the "ventriloquist" theory, for not even the finest ventriloquist in the world could sustain a note for twenty-four beats without showing at least a movement of the chest. Other things, too, made this theory untenable.

And so we came away from the sitting, leaving the investigator and the medium quite bright, alert, and not a bit tired after three hours of it. On the way home I asked the others " What do you make of it?" and they each replied, in his or her own way, "I'm blessed if I know: I can't make it out : there seems no possibility of fraud." And so we left it at that, for the time being.

CHAPTER VI

Interviewing a Soul
A UNIQUE EXPERIENCE
(G.A.W.)

As a journalist, I have on very many occasions been assigned the job of interviewing more or less distinguished people. The modus operandi is invariably the same. An appointment is made: the interviewer proceeds to the hotel or home of the person to be interviewed, having previously, perhaps, thought out a subject, or series of subjects, upon which to question the lady or gentleman, as the case may be. And having been ushered into his or her presence, the interviewer, usually, is greeted cordially, and after preliminaries, produces his notebook and begins.

What does Mr. So-and-So think of New Zealand? Has he had any interesting experiences since he left home? What were the conditions in the countries he has visited?—and scribble, scribble goes the pencil; and the busy brain of the journalist pieces together his "story" even as he jots down scattered notes. Often the interviewed is difficult to "draw." He, or she, has to be prompted; is diffident, or unimaginative, or very English. Sometimes, however, it is the opposite, and material flows from him or her through the brain and pencil of the lucky interviewer. It is a case of "Well, what do you want to know next?"

So that when Mr. Chapman said he would "try and arrange an interview" for me with friends "on the other side" for the purposes of this book, and did so arrange it, I was rather puzzled to know whether I should proceed on the same lines as I would do in the case of an earthly subject. However, I went out to "The Blue Room" with my note-book in my pocket, and a few leading questions in my mind, but I must confess, without any great expectations of a "story."

This is what happened.

Mr. Chapman, Mrs. Chapman (his mother), Miss Judd (the medium), and I were the only ones present. Mr. C. presided at the piano as usual; the medium sat in the corner of the room behind her little blue-draped table; while Mrs. Chapman and I occupied seats at either side of the fire-place. A hymn was first played ("The Day Thou Gayest," I think it was), and presently Dorothy's sweet mezzosoprano voice came through singing in unison with the piano. Next a few words of greeting from and to Dorothy, Wee Betty, and Charlie. It was at once noticeable that the voices were all much more distinct than usual, and the unseen visitors seemed to be much nearer. Indeed, at times during the evening, I had the feeling that if I looked up from my note-book I would see the one I was speaking with sitting or standing within hand clasp of me. Conditions were evidently ideal for this important occasion.

"Well, Charlie," I began, "we're going to have a real interesting talk tonight, I hope."

"I hope so," said Charlie.

"It was very good of you all to arrange this for me; it will mean a great thing for Clive's book,"
(Clive being Mr. Chapman).

Oh! that's all right; we're only too glad to help. It means a lot to us, too, you know."

Charlie then added that they would put Wee Betty (as the one having the most distinct voice) forward to answer the questions, it being understood that she would refer to him or to the others if she was unable to supply any particular answer herself. Charlie also indicated that there was a host of souls gathered round to listen. Just imagine it—I could visualise it all at the moment—our little band of friends gathered there, with Wee Betty eager and feeling quite important, in front, while all around and above them were perhaps thousands of souls waiting to see and to hear this strange performance. I myself realised that this was indeed a unique occasion, and that I was privileged to be the first newspaper man in the world to interview officially, for reporting purposes, and "voice to voice," as 'twere, a visitor from "The Land Beyond the Skies." I have heard of no other such interview, at any rate.

And so I began questioning Wee Betty, who remarked in her bright way that she thought I ought to address her as "Lady Betty," so important did she feel, my first question being "What is it like over there, Betty; have you scenery, flowers, and such like just as we have here?" And in her clear, childish, but intelligent way, she told me that there was scenery, very beautiful scenery, with delightful flower gardens. "We couldn't do without flowers, you know, Uncle George," my little subject remarked, "but our gardens aren't fenced in like yours. The flowers 'over there' are more-she puzzled for an expression—'more waxy like' than earth flowers, but they grow and develop much on the same lines, and require love and attention. You concentrate on a patch just like a farmer turns over the soil, and if you have a great desire for any particular kind of flower, that kind will grow for you. And there are not so many weeds here as you've got, either," added Betty.

"And what about buildings? Some folks say you have houses over there."

"Oh, yes," she explained, "we have houses of a kind; it's nice to live in one sometimes for a change; but they're not stuffy brick and stone houses like yours. They're 'desire houses,' and we like to visit each other just as real friends do on earth."

"And could you find anyone I asked you to find for me; any relation of mine, or friend?"

"Oh, Uncle George, have a heart. You must know there are millions and millions of souls over here; we can't know every one. Supposing you were going on a visit to Scotland," said this small Betty, "and I said to you, 'Ask for John McDonald, he is somewhere in Scotland, and give him my love,' that would be a job for you, wouldn't it?"

"I suppose it would, Betty," I agreed, and then asked, "Do you have your circle of particular friends there, as we have here?"

"Oh! yes," replied Betty, "But we all love each other. We speak to one another as we pass, and are drawn to some just as you are drawn to some people and not to others. Then we have a talk and tell each other our stories."

"Oh! I say"—and the irrepressible young soul went off at a tangent, as was her wont, "did you hear the cannon shot the other night, Uncle George?" Then she began to sing "I want to be Happy "-a song in the musical play "No, No, Nanette." I was puzzled for a few moments as to what she meant; then it dawned upon me. A few nights before this, Mr. Chapman had visited my home, and while we were in the sitting room and the gramophone was playing the record "I Want to be Happy," there was a loud knock, apparently just outside the window, which is well away from the street and high off the ground. We investigated but could find nothing or nobody, and Mr. Chapman laughingly suggested that "It must have been that little ticket, Betty."

"Was it you, Betty?" I asked now, but she laughed and said "I ain't goin' to tell."

Asked as to their work on the other side, Betty said that they were portioned off in bands to do rescue work and "all sorts of helpful things." They received their orders from "The Captain," just like in the army. At present, the band of which she was a member was portioned off to keep in touch with this world; in the meantime they did not go to other parts.

I have my own ideas as to thought forces, so I asked Betty whether, "over there," objects could be created, or materialised, by thought.

"Yes," she replied quickly; "that's right, Uncle George; you think a beautiful thought and beautiful things appear."

"Do you communicate by thought, then?" I asked.

"Yes, when we want to reach anyone a long way off : like a telephone you know. Thoughts can carry millions of miles, I should say, but we have an ordinary chat when we're together; you've heard us, haven't you?

Betty went on to explain that they were always learning "over there," just as we are here. Teachers came to them from higher spheres; met them at certain places, talked to them, and then went back.

The gatherings were mostly very big ones. "It's just like a minister and his congregation," volunteered Betty, "only we don't sit solemn with long faces and then go outside and say 'Didn't so-and-so have a pretty hat on?'; or 'Did you see Susie's new shoes?'; or 'I saw Mr. Such-and-such there, he hasn't paid my bill yet.' " "A lot of you people down there," added this little oracle, "Sit and listen to a sermon and say 'What a wonderful preacher!' but when you're asked what the preacher said, you cannot tell. " Here she gave a characteristic little laugh.

"I believe you have some sort of machines 'over there' with which you do certain of your work; is that so?"

"Yes; we have great machines in the rescue work; like aeroplanes or Zeppelins, with wings; shiny, silvery, and very bright. You would have to wear a mask to look at them, or it would hurt your eyes. They travel at a tre-men-dous rate; I expect they could go from here to London in a few minutes."

"Tell me, Betty," I said, "has each of us over here got a 'guardian angel'?"

"Most of you have each a 'messenger' at any rate, to inspire you to go on. The more spiritual and higher your thoughts, the more advanced is your messenger, they act as an inspiration."

"How do you locate us in this circle?"

"By the light it radiates; it's like a ray, or a searchlight. It is really a 'Ray of Love,' for love, you know, is the brightest vibration. We all need love," added Betty, "and when things go wrong with our loved ones over on your side it affects us here. We get 'mixed thoughts' then, and see little streaks, like spiders' webs. This distresses us, and then those from the higher spheres come through and talk to us, and then strong thoughts scatter the web and we're all right again."

"Just like a strong personality on this side coming along when things look black for us, and dissipating our worries and anxieties?" I suggested.

"That's just it, Uncle George. And when people are very obstinate or ignorant and won't accept the advice of the wise ones, it is better just to close down and come again when conditions are better—when the love vibrations begin again." (Scientists would do well to note this last sentence).

"There is one thing that I cannot quite understand," I remarked, "and that is the 'worldly nature' of your conversation with us; and 'up-to-date' songs, and the more or less superficial talk." ("Goodness; that's a big word," Betty chipped in here.)

"Oh! well," she explained; after consulting one of the others (we could hear them conversing in low tones); "we try and come down to your state; you know, we want to be friendly, just as if we were in the body and at a party. It is to let you see we are really very little different here, for a while anyhow. But when we have done our duty in that way we go back to our own sphere."

"And what do we look like to you, Betty?"

"Oh! it depends on how near we are to you. If conditions are favourable we get quite close and you look just as you'd look to your own folk; and if conditions are not good we see you as though you were in a mist. Only, if you are very good we see your souls; almost see what you are thinking. So, see that you have a good soul. It pays to be good, anyway, doesn't it?"

Betty went on to state that their "bodies" were illuminated bodies; much brighter than ours—"You know; you'd think we had electric lights in us, like glow-worms. " Their size was much the same as ours, but increased when they rose to the higher spheres' Sahnaei, for instance, was "extra high." But that did not mean, she added, that they went on ever increasing, or else "you'd think we were big telegraph poles or something."

Here Betty suggested that we might have a song, "to vary the thing a bit," and Jimmy sang a sailor ditty very nicely. Then I chose "Sad Little Eyes," and Nellie's voice immediately took up the strain, and at the conclusion of the song I asked Nellie if she remembered that it was just twelve months since she went over, and she replied, "Is it really."

Answering my questions, she said she remembered vividly those of whom she had been fond, or had thought a lot of. Some of her world memories were vivid, others not. Some things seemed a long way off, others very recent. "You will all realise it some day," she concluded. Her voice was particularly clear this night, and she appeared to be right in the room with us.

"What's worth having is worth waiting for," says Betty.

Then Dorothy came and sang "Beautiful Garden of Roses," and while she was conversing with Mr. Chapman, we could distinctly discern the scent of roses in the room. More songs were sung, each singer afterwards chatting for a few moments with one of us in the usual way, and then Charlie indicated that the proceedings were at an end.

"Good Night; God Bless You," said each of our friends in turn, and we bade them "Good Night." The final hymn, "Nearer My God to Thee," was sung by the band, and then silence.

So my interview ended. A far more interesting and satisfactory interview than the one, for instance, which I had with Sir Arthur Conan Doyle on the occasion of his visit to Dunedin. Sir Arthur, I remember, appeared to be worried, and was distrait, and all he could grant me was a few minutes talk in the vestibule of the Grand Hotel. I also remember that his remarks on that occasion appealed to my sense of humour rather than aroused my interest.

But in those days I had had no first-hand experience in the matter of communicating with the unseen world. Now, although I still retain my sense of humour (Thanks be!), I also realise that this particular subject is one which deserves to be treated in just as reverent a manner, and to be taken just as seriously, as does the subject of any more orthodox faith or religion.

CHAPTER VII
"Routine-Keeping Intelligence"

DISTINGUISHED SCIENTIST'S WARNING. (G.A.W.)

Away back in the early days in England, there was an old lady who, on being shown a cablegram and told that it was a message from her son across the sea, sent that very day over thousands of miles of wire, refused to receive it; to listen to any explanation concerning it, or to believe that it could be anything else but "the work of the devil." It was impossible for this dear old lady's mind, which had been trained in the good, straight and narrow path of orthodoxy from childhood, to accept or recognise anything so suggestive of "black magic." She had lived her life along well-defined lines in quiet rural England; lines which her mother and her grandmother had followed in their sweet and quaint old crinoline way. So when the wonderful cablegram set the villages chattering, the dear old lady retired to her room and prayed and prayed that no evil should befall those innocent folk of the village as the result of this terrifying thing.

I read of this incident a little while ago, and could understand the dear old lady's mind. Even to this day such minds are with us, and are made abundantly manifest in connection with Spiritualism and its investigations concerning the "other side." "The churches have taught us such and such," these folks say, "and have not so-called spiritualists been exposed as frauds? Away with it: we will not listen it is the work of the devil."

Yes, dear ladies and gentlemen, old and young; "Spiritualists" have been exposed; but, may I ask, in all tenderness, have not certain ministers of the gospel been found guilty of unchristian conduct? And, if we could but look into the minds of so-called religious devotees, would we not find many of them anything but sure of their faith? In other words, are there not millions of crass hypocrites in the world who, by reason of their outward seeming, cannot be unmasked and denounced? Of course there are. There are bad Christians; bad Mohammedans; bad Spiritualists. But there are also good and true Christians; good and true Mohammedans; good and true Spiritualists.

It was the scientist, Prof. Charles Richet, who, in his book Thirty Years of Psychical Research, says: " The history of all sciences warns us that the simplest discoveries have been rejected a priori as being incompatible with science. Medical anaesthesia was denied by Majendie. The action of microbes was contested for twenty years by all the scientists of all the academies. Galileo was imprisoned for saying that the earth revolved. Bouilland declared that the telephone was but ventriloquism. Lavoisier said that stones cannot fall from the sky, because there are no stones in the sky. The circulation of the blood was admitted only after forty years of sterile discussion. In a lecture in 1827, at the Academy of Sciences, my great grandfather,

P. S. Girard, considered it folly that water could be led to the upper floors of houses by pipes . In 1840, J. Miller declared that the speed of nerve impulses could never be measured. In 1699, Papin constructed the first steam-boat; a hundred years later, Fulton rediscovered the possibility of steam navigation, but it was not applied till twenty years later still. When in 1892, under the guidance of my distinguished master, Marey, I wade my first attempt in aviation, I met with only in-credulity, contempt, and sarcasm. A volume might be written on the absurd criticisms with which every great discovery has been received. Among the discoveries which by reason of my advanced age I have seen developed under my own eyes, so to speak, I will take four which in 1875 would have seemed ab-surdly inadmissible:

(1) The voice of an individual speaking in Paris can be heard in Rome (telephone).

(2) The germs of all diseases can be bottled and cultivated in a cupboard (bacteriology).

(3) The bones of a living person can be photographed (X-Rays).

(4) Five hundred guns can be taken through the air at a speed of 180 miles an hour (aeroplanes).

Anyone who uttered such audacities in 1875 would have been thought a dangerous lunatic. Our routinekeeping intelligence is such that it rejects anything to which it is unaccustomed."

Therefore, ladies and gentlemen—churchgoers or non-churchgoers, whichever you be—why not be tolerant, and at least "Wait and See"? There are many like my friend Clive Chapman, who are working quietly, diligently and devoutly, and making steady progress towards their goal. It is more than likely that within a few years the receiving of messages from our spirit friends by direct voice communication will no longer be regarded as phenomenal; it will be recognised, maybe, as an every day occurrence, just as radio messages are every day occurrences at the present. So, at least, give the investigators credit for being as true to their faith as you yourselves are to yours.

CHAPTER VIII
Puzzling It Out

"EXPLANATIONS" ELIMINATED
(G.A.W.)

Naturally, not being one who is easily "carried away" by unusual or strange happenings, I began, after my first visit to
"The Blue Room," to puzzle things out. I accepted nothing
completely, but reasoned each phase out, seeking a solution.
Since then, I have attended perhaps a dozen sittings, and although I have eliminated as impossible many of the explanations put forward by doubters, I have yet to find a reasonable
one with which to combat Mr. Chapman's confident asser-
tion that it is "the real thing." To make sure that mechanical
or wireless devices had nothing to do with the production, I
invited Mr. Chapman, his niece, his mother, and others interested to my own home. They willingly came (as they willingly
visit the homes of others who are genuinely interested), and
the results obtained were practically the same as those obtained in "The Blue Room" itself. Here again, from where I
sat, I was in a position to watch closely the mouth, throat,
and general demeanour of the medium, and once more failed
to discern the slightest movement that could indicate the production of the voices by ventriloquism.

And in respect to this "explanation" of ventriloquism (which
has, I might say, been put forward with confidence by more
than one intelligent citizen and visitor) I might add that a recent experience of mine disposes of it still more effectively.

On one or two occasions when Miss Judd was unable to ac-
company her uncle he brought with him another lady, one
who had been in the habit of attending the circles, and who,
in his opinion, possessed distinctly psychic powers. A young
man, also of the psychic type, was another of the party when
they thus visited my home one night. Having previously obtained slight results through this medium, Mr. Chapman suggested we should try again. We did so; this lady standing
behind the piano, the young man sitting on one side of Mr.
Chapman (who played the instrument), and I on the other;
thus forming a small, compact, and complete circle. After a
while faint voices were heard harmonising with the airs being
played. They were not nearly so loud nor so continuous as on
the occasions when Miss Judd was present; they came in
waves, so to speak, and at "the peak" were quite clear and of
beautiful quality. Instrumental accompaniments were heard
also, mellow 'cello tones being prominent.

At first I declined to accept this new evidence, for there remained the possibility (so faint were the voices at the outset)
that it might merely be the echo of the piano notes, or the vibration of the piano strings. But later, when a wave came as I
have described, there was no doubt that the voices were there,
and that they were unconnected with any echo.

Another possible explanation was that Mr. Chapman possessed hypnotic powers. Strange things have been done by
persons thus possessed. I have witnessed numbers of performances, many of them on the stage, and a few obviously spuri-
ous. But, after being in the company of Mr. Chapman for

one, evening, let alone a score of evenings, no one with any powers of observation, or who was a student of human nature at all, could have the slightest doubt that hypnotism had nothing whatever to do with it. Mr. Chapman is something of a dreamer, possessing insight, faith in abundance, and a yearning to convince the world of the existence of a future life; but he is obviously not possessed of that cheap brand of personal magnetism that lends itself to showmanship or charlatanism. He is, I feel sure, striving not after "spiritualistic phenomena," but to obtain evidence of after-life that will convince the world of the truth of Christianity—the essence of which the churches somehow seem to miss—and of the futility of the sin and selfishness which, if persisted in will drive it to an inevitable destruction.

Of the contentions put forward by those good conventional folk who refuse to accept anything that might disturb their set ideas of "Heaven," contentions which connect any manifestations such as these I am endeavouring to describe, with "the devil," or something of the kind, we need take little heed. The same type of folk have taken the same attitude all down the ages concerning anything new—steam, electricity, telephones, wireless, X-Rays, submarines, etc. Yet they accept without reserve and without requiring any explanation, the miracles recorded in the Bible, miracles of which the very explanation must be a psychic one.

It may be mentioned that amongst those who have attended circles with Mr. Chapman and Miss Judd are ministers of religion, Divinity and other students, doctors, professors and scientists, actors and actresses, newspaper men, commercial men, tradesmen, professional and amateur conjurers, magicians and ventriloquists, in addition to orthodox spiritualists, phenomena seekers, and investigators generally. And at least 95 per cent of them have gone away either bewildered or else thoroughly convinced of the genuineness of the manifestations. A small percentage have harboured doubts, but even these have been unable to put forward a tenable theory or feasible explanation.

CHAPTER IX.
IN CONCLUSION

"THINK IT OUT FOR YOURSELF"
(G.A.W.)

So, dear reader, there you have an outline of what can scarcely fail to appeal to you as at least a marvelous development of communication with the unseen world. You may ask, seeing that I have taken upon myself a big share in the placing of these revelations before you, "What is your own opinion?" As a comparative newcomer into the circle; as a newspaper man who is accustomed to take any unusual or strange story "with a grain of salt"; as one who is inclined to search out the truth of a matter rather than to blare it forth for the sake of the sensation it will cause; and as one who has studied and endeavoured (with as much success as is possible with the average weak mortal) to bring into practice the teaching of Prentice Mulford and other leaders in what is known as the New Thought Movement, I can, after giving the matter deep thought and consideration, and investigating it as thoroughly as I have been capable of doing; I can honestly say, "I think there is a whole lot in it."

You may, if you wish, eliminate from your calculations the automatic writing, sketching, and the like. Into this there is always the possibility of the influence of the human medium's mind entering. At the same time, I have seen excellent sketches of heads and faces drawn by people who assured me they had never at any time any pretensions to artistic ability.

Still, the opportunity to "fake" is there, so, if you wish, dismiss the automatic sketch and writing.

Then there is the table moving. This, too, has been "faked" by tricksters, but always in the dark. Personally, after experiencing the force-directing powers described in the earlier pages of this book, I cannot agree with the scornful ones who dismiss the matter with the remark "Trickery." Who was the trickster?—Mr. Chapman, a short, slightly built, anything but muscular, anything but "tricky" individual? Miss Judd, a young girl of nineteen, with the ordinary girl's lack of lifting power in the arms? It could not be a combination of Mr. Chapman and his niece, for I have seen the table rise when the latter was standing away from it. Was it Mrs. Chapman, an old lady of 65? Was it I? I'm certain there was no physical trickery, anyhow. If it was mind power; suggestion, or such like, well, matters are moving—literally moving—in that direction.

I confess I have not witnessed any manifestation of materialisation or de-materialisation. Knowing Mr. Chapman pretty thoroughly, I am prepared to believe his statements in this regard. I have had occasion to test his integrity, and have carefully noted the fact that he has in his intercourse with me, anyway, never "let his imagination run away with him."

He himself has a probing mind, an analytical mind, and a mind with a scientific bent. And, as one who has knocked up against a good many classes of people in a good many parts of the world, and been fooled (as most wanderers are) a good many times before learning my lesson, I will stake my reputation as something of a judge of the human species on my opinion of Clive Chapman, who is, I maintain, thoroughly earnest and thoroughly honest.

Well, now, there remains—if you decide not to take any chances with the automatic writing, or the automatic sketching, or the table turning, or the dematerialisation—there remains, I say, "the voices." How are you going to explain them; to silence them? I have disproved, I think, the explanations, or accusations, of ventriloquism, of hypnotism of wireless, or other mechanical means of trickery. The voices are there : distinctly heard in the brightly-lit room; talking intelligently with you; singing to you; even playing upon instruments for your entertainment or enlightenment.

What are they, then? Whence came they? If you won't admit the possibility of spirit voices coming across space, even though you do complain if the announcer in Sydney or Melbourne does not very clearly give the name of the winner of a race in the result of which you are interested; if you scoff at there being such things as spirits or souls, then you must find some other explanation. You may say that it is some wonderful discovery whereby thoughts are made audible, and that the medium or her mentor, or both, are the "intelligences" who are conversing with you.

This is a far-fetched theory, but as good, or as poor, a one as I have heard brought forward.

But if this, or a similar, explanation is the correct one; if it is all trickery, why does not Clive Chapman capitalise it, and, with his niece, Pearl Judd, tour Europe, Asia, Africa, America, and Australia, earning hundreds of pounds a week? Why, at the least, does he not advertise his "find," and charge admission to his sittings, and thus add to his nominal earnings as a tradesman? I think I can tell you why he refuses to make money out of this discovery. It is because he and his niece believe—they know—that they are but the humble instruments of the Great Unseen Powers who are using them for the purpose of helping this poor, selfish, sin-encrusted old world to see the error of its ways. That is what they believe. But whether the world will hear, or hearing, take notice of the still small voice crying from such a small and (in the eyes of the Greater Cities) insignificant centre as Dunedin, New Zealand, is questionable.

Yet Clive Chapman and Pearl Judd will, I am convinced, go on striving until they themselves "go over"; striving in order to bring peace and enlightenment to a world that has not overburdened them with favours or even kindnesses. Success to their labours, then, and may their highest hopes—which include the coming of the day when the outer world and this mortal world will be brought into visible contact—be realised. I can imagine the comfortably-waisted man of commerce remarking : "Perhaps; but I'll risk it," and resuming his eating and drinking and money-making.

I can imagine the orthodox church man warning his flock against "the works of the devil" (though there are growing up different opinions as to what and who are the devils and who are the saints of the world). But let the reader of this little book think it out for himself, and draw his own conclusions. But let him not forget that "there are more things in Heaven and Earth, Horatio, than are dreamt of in our philosophy."

CHAPTER X
Some Explanations
(By Clive Chapman)

Perhaps my readers may wonder how these dear souls come to be heard and not seen; why some are more easily heard than others, and what relation psychic power has to sound.

Well, to begin with, try and understand that vibrations are the foundation of everything; nothing can exist without vibration, which is movement, which is life. There are millions of scales of vibrations, and psychic power and sound are of such a rate that they can be combined, or in reality, one (sound) can be concentrated in the other (psychic power) so that those beyond are able to control the sound-waves to such an extent that they may speak to us through those waves. The more harmonious the sound-waves (or music) we produce on this side of The Veil, the more easily can these souls beyond control them. This will be understood without difficulty when one is listening to the voices, for it may then be noticed that certain chords or sustained notes invariably appear to give good results. Often when a piece of music is played over several times there is what might be termed a leveling of the tones and more than one voice heard at the same time : say a woman's voice and a man's.

Now, this can be explained by the fact that each voice is "tuned in" to the sound-wave most suitable to it, and the more perfect the chords the more clearly are the extra voices heard. Some of these extra voices are extremely delicate, and so not easy to hear, thereby proving of what a fine wave-length of sound, or vibration, they are composed compared with the sounds we produce. That, then, accounts for the length of time that it has been necessary to devote to the developing and perfecting of this method of communicating with the beyond, and also why just a band of chosen souls, as it were, have been sent forward to become well used to this method so that they might make themselves easily heard above the sound-waves produced on this side.

A piano is a good instrument to use, for many reasons, as several notes or tones are sounded together, so making it possible for those beyond to "tune in" better. Of course, as things stand at present, those on the other side have complete control, and can sing, talk, play instruments, etc., just as they wish, when there is perfect harmony all round. Everyone present must be friendly and in tune with each other, otherwise vibrations of another kind are set up and affect, perhaps destroy, the results.

The sooner the world realises the reality of vibrations, even of thoughts and their effects on a sensitive mind, the sooner will it know the true meaning of Life and Love, which is the highest vibration of all, being of God alone. This in time overpowers all other vibrations, which will fade out unless the highest vibration is allowed to penetrate them. I am not preaching when I write thus, but merely pointing out how real these vibrations are. To study vibrations properly the mind must be developed to a high state of sensitiveness, even to the state of being disturbed by the dropping of a pin. I am afraid this cannot be said of many scientists, who make far too much of ponderous material. A study of vibrations, faithfully carried out, must lead one to a sense of reason and deduction.

The mind itself is a most sensitive instrument, a thousand times more sensitive than the most delicate wireless instrument, and is capable of receiving impressions or thoughts from other minds beyond this world; minds still existing, remember, but free of the flesh, hence their ability to impress our minds, provided we but open them to receive the messages thus sent. We then direct the thought, by our mind, to our brain, which in turn controls the nerves concerned, and by which the act—be it speech, walking, eating, or anything else, is brought to its performance. Thus the thought becomes an action understood by everybody.

In inspirational work the mind is being directed by a greater mind from beyond which is anxious to put some work through such a sensitive instrument for the sake of helping and uplifting others. All the books in the world cannot teach you what a perfectly open mind can; because such a mind is tuned to receive the best thoughts from beyond, while a biased mind is crippled from the outset and simply repels a wealth of valuable material. This shows the desirability of raising the vibrations to as high a pitch as possible. This is the reason that true mediums, or instruments, are used by those beyond for the purpose of communicating with us. As a rule mediums are highly strung and easily affected, and those beyond, as it were play upon their vibrations, which also draw an excess of psychic power.

WHAT IS PSYCHIC POWER!

This psychic power is really a kind of atmosphere surrounding the medium and capable of expansion by development under the control of those beyond who have been appointed to the task in conjunction with any earnest and faithful investigator on this side. Psychic power, in its true sense, is not to be confused with the ectoplasm spoken of as being produced from mediums, but an invisible force capable of being controlled by those beyond and not affecting the medium in the slightest. In its pure ' state it is beyond the power of the medium, as it is not material as we know it, but a force penetrating and surrounding certain persons more than it does others. These persons we call mediums, or instruments, because they are, as it were, a channel of direction. Psychic power is in reality an exceedingly refined form of electricity—or what we call electricity but it is quite beyond the control of a human being.

I want my readers to make quite sure that they have grasped this fact—especially the scientists—because once they do so they will find that their investigations will go ahead far more rapidly. Get rid of the idea that the medium controls the power, as it is so often called, and try to understand that it is a "state of force" controlled by higher intelligences than ours, under properly arranged conditions, and is in reality around everybody. As conditions are developed, this force expands more freely around the real mediums, who are used as central points of "circles," in much the same manner as hydrogen gas expands in a rising balloon. Thus results become more extensive, just as our view of the surrounding country does from the balloon. It is this particular force that those beyond work through in order to get to us, as it is so extremely fine in its vibrations that any coarse vibrations, such as those produced by gloominess, anger, doubt, jealousy, material thoughts, etc., drown them out.

WHY INVISIBLE?

Those beyond are invisible to us simply because the substance of their world and of themselves is composed of vibrations far too rapid for our physical eyes to see; vibrations more rapid than light, which are the highest we can sense by sight.

Take, now, what is called the spectrum—that coloured band of light which is produced by splitting up white light into its different wave-lengths; the red end being the slowest and the blue, or ultra-violet, end the most rapid. Accepting the fact that the higher the life the more rapid the vibrations, it follows that investigators into the world beyond must use, on this side, means which will produce the most rapid that it is possible to produce, while those beyond gradually lower the rate of their vibrations in order to link up with us. The real psychic power is of a rate of vibration closely akin to the rate of those beyond, and under their control, it may easily be understood how they can come in contact with it when it is around a medium, get into touch with our rate of vibration, and so communicate with us although invisible themselves.

MEDIUMS

Most people see only the medium and do not understand that the real power is around and not in this medium. It is a blessing that most mediums have not control of the real psychic power, otherwise the whole world would soon be wrecked. This power is jealously guarded, and that is one reason why God has placed it around human beings instead of around, say a box, a jug, a stone column or any other inanimate object. If this had been done just imagine the amount of strife that would take place and the harm that would follow the possession by some people of the precious object. Whereas, being placed around a human being the power is safe, for unless the very essential conditions are strictly observed, no development of any value can take place. The human being has to be considered first in every case, and this is something that those beyond never fail to see to. They will not allow their instrument to be played with, and insist always that the medium shall be kept in a happy state of mind. This may be understood, as vibrations being real things, any unhappy mental state in the medium must set up a rate too heavy for those beyond to work through. I hope my readers see what I am driving at and will, if they investigate at all, investigate power and not mediums. Do not look upon a real medium, or psychic, as some curious creature, and remember that he or she is not superhuman or tireless, but may be easily ruined by careless or ignorant people. Treat the medium as a treasure

from God, but do not impress upon him or her the importance of his or her "gift," as it is often called. The power be-
longs to God, and is really around everybody, if they would
only wake up to the fact. If everyone would but have faith
and understanding how easily those beyond could come to us,
especially when so many means of communication are provided.

NOT EVERY SOUL CAN COME THROUGH

Many people expect to have their "dead" relatives come to
them at a sitting; but this is not always possible, as conditions
of all sorts may intervene. It depends upon what sphere the
particular relative whose presence is desired may be living on,
for every sphere is not tuned in to the same medium. Those,
therefore, who are enquirers only for the purpose of seeking
out their own relatives or friends must be prepared for possible disappointment, as they may never come into touch with
them at all on this side. Then, again, think of the countless
millions of souls who have passed over even during the last
two or three hundred years, and of the extreme difficulty
which the little band that comes to us would experience in
bringing along at a moment's notice anyone named to them.
Believe me, those souls have their time well occupied with
work, and they have their limitations, for they like we, are just
growing and developing all the time.

It must also be remembered that although these dear souls have now come to the stage of singing and speaking to us clearly and distinctly, every new soul trying to do the same through these vibrations of sound has to first learn the method, and usually begins very faintly and faultily. Therefore it is but rarely that a new soul comes through to us now, as this band have had to work hard to develop the power to enable them to be heard publicly and to prove to the world that those beyond are indeed alive, not "dead," by singing and talking to us. They are really a representative band sent to prove how real is this life beyond, and they depend on the faithful few on this side to keep the door open by means of this wonderful phase of sound-waves and psychic power combined, which has been developed during the past few years around my niece.

PHYSICAL FEATS NOT FAVOURED

I have heard many people say "Why don't these spirits do this or that?" referring to physical work. Some have actually asked could they help dig the garden, or lift a weight, not realising that those beyond do not come to do our work for us, but to encourage us to believe in an after life and to have sufficient faith to carry on in this life and not to allow troubles or worries to deaden our hearts.

It must be remembered that if our hands were made of a substance like steam, which is more dense than the substance of which the hands of those beyond is composed, we would not be able to grasp a chair or a stick and lift it. Why, then, ask them to do such things? It is only when conditions make it possible in a circle those on the other side can steady the vibrations sufficiently to allow them to concentrate their power into a sort of ray, which lifts and' moves material things; just as a jet of water or air can be used to move an article; except that the power they use is invisible. Then, again, we would become a lazier race if we had our work done thus for us, and what useful purpose would it serve to have objects moved just that we might see that it could be done? If we have faith—real faith—they will do a lot for us; but not on demand, only when it will serve a useful purpose.

CONTROL NOT IN HUMAN HANDS

These souls take full control of everything now and are unbending. And when one looks around the world today it is easy to understand their attitude. My niece is just their instrument for this particular method of demonstrating the life beyond, and they guard her from all misuse by operating just when they know it is best; they are of almost military strictness in this and will not come "just for fun." It is this "fun" that some people on earth and weak spirits beyond indulge in that leads to danger. Such people would do well to leave all psychic investigation alone; it should be taken up in all seriousness or not at all.

THE POWER OF FAITH

Just as a swimmer can get along easiest in smooth water, so can these dear souls make their voices heard best when the sound is smooth-flowing and all the persons in the room are in harmony with each' other. A discord, I have often noticed, breaks up the voice, unless the conditions are particularly good.

The tone of the voices, too, varies according to the class of instrument being played; when it is a gramophone the voice appears to be in the instrument and is thin or muffled. But when a violin is being played the voice sounds full and clear and almost as if floating in the air. When an organ is being played more than one or two voices are often heard together and very full.

But, I repeat, it is only to those who have real faith in these souls and in the life beyond that these fine and full results will come; so I hope and pray that the readers of this little book will, if ever they are given the opportunity of hearing these dear ones, extend to them an open welcome, and so pave the way for the best results. Remember, they will not come forward unless they are kindly received, any more than people on earth would; the atmosphere of love is essential to them. It is not an entertainment they are giving. At the sittings the voices are always faintly heard at first, so that those present may get used to the idea of not listening to the sound of the piano, or whatever instrument is being played, but to concentrate upon the voices alone, thereby compelling the attention which those from beyond expect from us here. As attention, sociability, and faith develop during a demonstration, so does the strength of the voices, until eventually, they are all distinctly heard.

GREATER AND DEEPER KNOWLEDGE COMING

Too much knowledge of a deep nature is not given to us by those who come in this band, for this reason They come first to gain the confidence of the people, and their friendship, by song and bright conversation. That is why Wee Betty is so often to the front; she is put forward because of her bright nature and high spirits. If people accept her the rest follow. And rarely indeed is she not warmly and lovingly welcomed. Knowledge of life and its lessons are often wrapped up in apparently jocular remarks by Wee Betty and others, this tone being evidently adopted to avoid the proceedings becoming too heavy or pedantic. But, I feel sure that once the attention of the world has been gained, the more serious and profound knowledge that is needed and is being anxiously looked for by many, will be forthcoming in the form of instruction by the more advanced teachers, who now merely wait until the conditions have been perfected for the clear and unmistakable delivery of this great message. This present band of workers with whom communication has been brought about may be looked upon as a scouting party, or pioneers, sent to blaze the path that will form the concluding link between this world and the next.

MERELY INSTRUMENTS

Finally, I want to impress upon my readers that neither my niece nor I take any credit whatever for our work in this movement; nor do we desire fame or publicity; being sure and certain that we are but instruments under the control of those beyond who are striving to thus prove the existence of ever-lasting life.

CHAPTER XI
Testimonies of Sitters

Here follow a few of the letters or "declarations" received by Mr. Chapman from people who have attended sittings at his home and elsewhere.

A HUSBAND AND BROTHER SPOKEN WITH

"For the last two or three years I have had the privilege of sitting in the circles with Mr. Chapman, his mother, and his niece (Miss Pearl Judd), in my own home and the homes of others. To me these sittings have been most beautiful and wonderful, for the singing, and playing on different instruments by those dear souls on the "other side" have been a real treat to listen to. Of my own personal experiences I claim to have spoken to my mother, who 'passed over' several years ago, my brother (Bob McLean), who 'passed over' four years ago, and also my husband, Horace Prattley, who was killed on the Somme, in the Great War. Besides speaking, it has been very comforting to be able to come in touch with my loved ones the way I do. On one or two occasions, I have experienced the power on the table; that is to say, a number of us gathered round the table and held it up; then those on 'the other side' used tremendous pressure on the table, the power being so strong at times that it took one all they knew to hold on. The strange part about it is that one person will feel the pressure while another close beside will feel nothing. I myself have stood between two others at the side of the table. While these two would feel the pressure, I would be getting nothing.

Then I would get it and they would get nothing. The table test alone is, I think, a great proof of the power of the Spirit. I may state that this particular band who come to us are also rescue workers; that is, they do rescue work on their side of life, helping along those who are in a little darkness. To me, that is a wonderful work too. Some time back Mr. Chapman held a rescue circle on a Sunday evening, and I had the privilege of sitting at it. First one (Wee Betty), sometimes two (she and Peter), and sometimes my own husband (when he wasn't on duty) would converse and sing with us while the others would be on the lower spheres, giving a helping hand to the weaker souls. On those occasions we would hear the distinct buzz of the 'engines' of the machines they use, as they were passing. These spirit friends of ours have given us quite a lot of information about the beauties of the Great Beyond.

(Signed) VIOLET PRATTLEY,
3 Miller Street,
St. Kilda, Dunedin

A SCEPTIC CONVINCED

"When I first heard it was possible to speak to our dear ones who had passed over to 'the other side,' I would not believe it, and used to say all sorts of things of the ones who were trying to persuade me that I could hear voices coming through a medium. Then it was arranged that my wife and myself should have a circle in our own home, and to our great surprise, everything happened just as we were told it would.

We heard some beautiful singing, and also lovely music played on string and wind instruments, and my wife and I thoroughly enjoyed the evening. The more we heard of it the more interested we became, and now I am quite convinced that it is possible to hear from our loved ones, who have passed to 'the other side.' I must say Mr. Chapman has done wonders with this work during the time he has spent on it. I will say that the circle has been held in our home several times, and both my wife and I have spoken to my brother, who was killed in the War in 1917, and I declare that I knew his voice the moment he spoke to me; also that of my wife's brother, who came through very plainly.

(Signed) E. A. THURSTON

A MILTON PARTY

"With a party of friends from Milton, I had the pleasure of paying a visit to the 'Blue Room.' There was nothing eerie, or uncanny about the room, and certainly nothing calculated to aid or harbour deception. Yet that modestly furnished sitting-room contains more mystery than the most ingenious imagination could conceive. It offers a straightforward and weird puzzle that my thirty years of ventriloquial and magical experience do not help to solve. The medium was seated in a corner of the room, and throughout the evening she remained there in full view of everyone present; but beyond an occasional smile and a passing glance of interest, she took no part in the proceedings Mr. Chapman softly played the piano, the medium waited silently, and the visitors listened with eager attention. A few minutes passed without result, then faintly above the music the voice of a man was heard singing. With gradually increasing strength the singing grew louder until, at the close of the song, it was distinctly audible to every person in the room. 'That's Charlie,' said Mr. Chapman, with the evident familiarity of one who was intimately acquainted with the Unseen. 'Hullo, Charlie,' he said, gazing at a section of the floor between the fireplace and himself.

'Hullo,' said the voice.

The piano tinkled away and a fascinating conversation was carried on between this intensely serious man and the Voice. It was interrupted by another voice—that of a child—who laughingly demanded that the pianist should play 'something with a little ginger in it.' The melody changed, and the child's voice sang a nice little ditty, interspersed with childish chatter to various persons in the room. Gradually other voices joined the invisible company until a unique concert party seemed to have assembled in the atmosphere between the medium and the visitors. First there was 'Charlie,' a splendid tenor singer, who sang several songs, and acted as chief spokesman of the company. Next was 'Wee Betty,' a veritable child comedienne. (Comic songs, patter, and witty remarks). 'Dorothy,' a splendid mezzo-soprano, and someone else who played a violin. A cornet and violoncello were also in evidence. Songs, duets, and instrumental items were rendered in first-rate style. Everything was done in the 'Blue Room' under the most satisfying conditions. The visitors, with all their faculties alert, listened, with might and main, but nothing suspicious was in any way apparent, or even suggested. Mr. Chapman explained that the spirit voices came on the sound waves through the medium, and that the stopping of the music broke the 'connection.' If it was a ventriloquial deception, a second visit to the 'Blue Room' did not help me to detect it. If it was ventriloquism, Mr. Chapman has discovered something which will bring fame and fortune to his feet without imposing on the credulity of a few visitors who are anxiously seeking for truth.

No, ventriloquism does not explain the phenomenon of the 'Blue Room,' and Milton visitors are no wiser than before. Perhaps another party of visitors will be wiser—and perhaps not.

(Signed) EDWARD YOUNG
MRS.E.YOUNG
JAS.W.ANDERSON
P.C.FARRELL
J.SCOON.G.W.LANE

MILTONIANS AGAIN IMPRESSED

"On the evening of 17th October, 1927, at the residence of Mr. Chapman, in Musselburgh, Dunedin, we, the undersigned residents of Milton, witnessed an exhibition of table lifting phenomena. We were first arranged round a large dining table in a brightly lighted room, Miss Judd the medium at one end, Mr. Chapman at the other, while three of us were placed on either side. At Mr. Chapman's request we placed our fingers under the edge of the table and raised it slightly from the floor. In a few moments a downward pressure was applied from some invisible source to different parts of the table in turn. An obvious invitation to participate was then extended to two of the members of the party who had been standing out. The request was complied with and pressure was again applied. Suddenly the table was raised to a height of about seven feet, remaining about two inches below the electric light bulb, our fingers making the slightest possible contact under the edge. The table descended to its previous position and rocked violently. A young girl of about 9 or 10 years seated herself on the table, which we raised as before, no additional weight being apparent. Again the table was elevated by the invisible force, and once more it descended, to rock violently as though to throw off its fair young burden.

On the young lady getting off we once more lifted the table clear of the floor, and again it was raised to full height. Mr. Chapman requested 'Trevor' to give us an aeroplane stunt, and the table at once swooped down and across the room till the legs nearly grazed the floor when it began to rise again. Although the speed of the descent had been such as to make us imagine the table would crash through the wall, its motion was checked and stopped before the person at the end was squeezed against the wall. For quite half an hour these and similar inexplicable phenomena kept us in a state of bewilderment. We were, for example, completely at a loss to explain the origin of the extraordinary force that was applied in an attempt to force a member of our party to sit on a couch.

Certainly it would have been impossible for Miss Judd and Mr. Chapman to exert so much force without showing evidence of the strain. One of the most remarkable and most baffling features of the entertainment, if it may be so called, was the fact that nothing in the room except the table was displaced. So violent were the table's movements that we were kept in a continual state of suspense. It seemed as though it would be impossible eventually to avoid causing some accident. Yet on each occasion the table would stop, apparently cushioned, sufficiently far from the wall or light bulb to avoid damage, not even the smallest and lightest ornaments being moved. Some power the nature of which we cannot conceive was evidently at work, for there were no visible means of controlling the table.

(Signed) P. C. FARRELL
D. M. DONALD
F. J. SHERWOOD
P. J. GREY

THEOLOGICAL STUDENT'S OPINION

The following accounts were written by a Presbyterian theological student. He did not write his impressions of his first visit.

This (13/3/27) was my second visit to Mr. Chapman's. I went out with Dr. and Mrs. G_. The former met the company and then left for a meeting in town—to return an hour later. There were present—Clive Chapman, Miss Pearl Judd (the medium), Miss_ , Miss_ , Mrs. G. and myself.

The first thing we did was to stand round the dining-roam table and lift it slightly from the floor. In a very short time several of us felt distinct pressure on the table over our hands. An interesting and remarkable feature of this phenomena was that one would feel the pressure, while the person standing right alongside would notice nothing except the ordinary weight of the table. Clive declared that throughout his right hand was severely pressed, while his left was unaffected. I can personally vouch for the fact of increased pressure. It was most marked. Clive and I tried a few experiments. We found that the pressure exerted by the "force" was as great as that exerted by one of us resting our whole weight upon the table. Various other occurrences took place, including divers rotatory and spiral movements of the table. I noticed, however, that if I exerted great strength I could prevent much movement at times.

We then moved into the room in which the sittings are held. As before there was a good fire in the grate, three lights on, and the whole room done in blue. In one corner, away from the fire, sat Miss Judd. Opposite her, the two girls and A.C.W. sat. Mrs. G. occupied the chair on the other side of the fire opposite the piano, which Clive played throughout.

Not more than thirty seconds from the commencement of the music a voice was heard singing the air. Soon the voice said "Righto." Personally, I had no difficulty in recognising this voice again. It was quite distinctive with a peculiar inflexion. He has a way of hesitating over a word occasionally when he speaks. The amazement with which I heard this voice on the first occasion was absent, and one commenced talking to him in a perfectly natural way. All present greeted him as "Charlie," and he spoke to several. After observing the phenomena I should prefer to call him the Censor. It seemed to me that his conversation was limited in some way, and I had the impression that this was determined by the mentality of the circle.

It was not long before the voice of "Betty" came through, and very distinctly too. Her voice seemed to be right in the middle of the room and was as clear as the voices of those present. Anyone who had listened to her voice for the greater part of an evening, as I had done last year, simply could not fail to recognise it again. It is in all senses of the word a child's voice. Through the interplay of conversation one has the impression of a distinct personality—as real as that produced by a conversation on the telephone. The following dialogue took place:

Betty: "Hullo, Mrs. G. I haven't seen you for a long time. I'm so glad that you are back again."

Mrs. G.: "Good evening Betty—yes, it is good to be back and to hear your voice. Is there anyone else here that you know?"

117

Betty: "Ha-a-a! Ha-a-a-a!" (this was said in a very funny way—so characteristic of Betty, who is full of fun). "My sheik, some sheik, eh what?"

Mrs. G.: "What else did you call him?"

Betty: "Don't make me blush—'Valentino'—Hullo Betty, hullo Mamie (to the two girls next to me), Hullo Rudy."

It was quite apparent that Betty was speaking to me, but no one quite understood the significance of her new nickname. Finally it dawned upon us—"Rudolf Valentino." On the previous occasion she had called me "Valentino," which she shortened to 'Tiny,' and made great fun over my height.

Mrs. G.: "Do you know where the other sheik has gone ? "

(This referred to Mr. G , who had introduced me to Clive, and whom Betty had called her sheik.)

Betty: "Oh, he's a wanderer still—over the water somewhere." (G. had left for Australia.)

A.C.W.: "Have you spoken to us since we were last here?"

Betty: "Of course. Don't you remember the time I made the table climb up on to your knee. It was a long climb, Rudy, but it was worth it when I got there."

Mrs. G.: "Which room did we use, Betty?"

Betty: "The old room—and I came to you three or four times."

This is interesting as only Mrs. G. and I knew of the incident of the table to which Betty referred. Her description was accurate. At the time we were using the table in the front room.

Charlie : "It's very nice to see you again, Mrs. G"

Mrs. G.: "Do you think it's any good our using the table?"

Charlie: "Rather"—(a common word on his lips). "It is good practice for those on this side."

A.C.W.: "Do you remember that I asked you to find several people for me?"

Charlie : "Yes, but I haven't come across them yet. But I am sure we will before long—perhaps next time you come."

Betty: "Never say die till the dead horse kicks you"

At this point Charlie sang his first song of the evening, at the request of the company. A little later he introduced us to "Jim." He is the brother of Miss Reid, and he died when he was a small child.

Betty: "Jim, this is Mrs. G._and there's Rudy. Look at him—he has only a chair to love." (I had my left arm round a chair, which was reserved for Dr. G.). "Look out. I might come over there and climb up the 'mountain.' I see you noticed my lips, Rudy. "

This last statement is rather interesting. Before commencing the sitting Clive showed us two pencil drawings of a small girl of about 7 or 8 years of age. This was done by Miss Judd after the manner of automatic writing. The drawings were excellent. While looking at them I said "She has given herself a good pair of lips."

Betty: "And I can use them too. Here you are, Mrs. G." (and at that came a loud "smack." To those familiar with the sound there was no mistaking it.) "I do like your wee baby, Mrs. G."

Mrs. G.: "Do you know who is looking after her tonight ? "

Betty : "Auntie—and you be sure to bring her the next time you come. I mean Auntie." (This referred to Miss S., whom, of course, only Mrs. G. and I know.)

Charlie sang again. He was accompanied by a violin. Then Jim sang. His voice was not nearly so distinct. He was followed by a cornet solo, which to my mind was one of the most remarkable events of the evening. It was so obviously a cornet, and it came through very clearly, sounding much more natural than a similar instrument over the wireless. "Dorothy" (whom we had met previously) sang with her deep contralto voice, but every now and then the sound faded out. After she had finished Charlie and she carried on a conversation about the conditions. Charlie thought there was something wrong with the piano. I seemed to be the only one who heard this talk. I broke in upon the conversation, whereupon Betty said, "So you're eavesdropping, too. " Betty sang several songs. Mrs. G. asked her if she knew the gramophone record of "Bo Peep." This was familiar to her, and she spoke of the "wee records." In singing the songs " Comin' Through the Rye" and the "Bonnie Banks of Loch Lomond" she made her voice trill, as children do, when imitating sheep-the Ba-a-a-a touch.

The next to "appear" was "Peter." He spoke to those present who knew him, but I said that I had not met him before. This was the reply I got—" Of course you have, but it's all right—you're in love. "

Peter sang a song as a schoolboy of about 12 would sing, and he was helped out on his top notes by Charlie, with a little "help" also from the inimitable Betty. After the song Betty started again in his way.

"Would you like me to tell you a joke?" We said we would.

"Do you know how a man keeps a birthday?"

"No."

"He takes the day off."

"But do you know how a woman keeps a birthday?"

"She takes two years off."

The conversation became general, but after a few minutes I asked Betty if I could ask her a question. During the whole sitting I had my notebook on my knee and wrote most of the time. What I here record is a part, but a typical part of the conversation and events. When Betty said I could ask a question I prepared to write,

Betty: "Right, sec."

A.C.W.: "I should like to know how you live where you are. Do you have something like what we call families?"

Betty : "No, we don't live like that—we just keep with the people we like—we are all like one big family—and then we can go round visiting the people we want to visit."

A.C.W.: "But perhaps they don't want you to visit them. "

Betty : "They are just as anxious to know you as you are to know them—(these words were said very slowly and deliberately). Of course, it is hard to explain just what it's like. I am only giving you the A.B.C. of it all."

A.C.W.: "Now then, can I ask you another question?"

Betty : "Just a moment I will try to make a long face.

A.C.W.: "Well, are we set?"

Betty : "No, it's no good, my face won't set."

A.C.W.: "Can you tell me why it is so hard to get names through from the other side?"

Betty: "But it's not"—(and then she rattled off about a dozen names very quickly—they ranged from Robinson Crusoe and Queen Elizabeth to Charlie Chaplin.) When she used the last name she said, "But he hasn't come over here yet. How many more names do you want?"

A.C.W.: "But you don't quite understand what I mean. We have found it is very difficult to get names by means of the table."

Betty : "Wait a moment, I'll ask Charlie"—(they both commenced to explain).

"Hullo, here's someone coming." (No one the room had heard anything, but it had been arranged that when Dr. G. returned he should slip in the front door and come straight into the front room where we were sitting.)

Betty: "Come in."

She repeated this several times, the last time fairly shouting it. Dr. G. walked in, having heard her voice in the hall quite clearly. This was his first experience of this type of phenomenon, and he showed remarkable savoir faire in his sitting down and commencing a conversation with a voice "from the air."

Betty : "Hullo Doc.—had a nice evening?"

Charlie sang "Songs of Araby," greatly to the delight of Dr. G. These two carried on quite an extended conversation about music and its possibilities and use on the other side. Jim also played the violin for the doctor's sake. Betty said they didn't like jazz, which was "like a horse going thumpety-thumpety down the street, it never changes; the softest music is the best."

I recommended my series of questions about the difficulty of getting names through the table. Charlie said there were usually a great number of spirits who tried to get through to us and the vibrations got mixed. Betty thought communication by means of the direct voice was much better. She did not like "this business of 1, 2, 3, 4 taps" and so on.

I asked Charlie if they played anything that corresponded to our games. I did this for the purpose of leading up to questions about memory, its lasting effects, its relation to the spirit, and the value of reading and study. Charlie did not give me much information on these points, which after all are of vital importance in any conception of a continued existence. He said that they didn't have "games," and that one forgot a great deal of what happened on the earth. It was very difficult to explain—perhaps I could get someone else to explain what I wanted. He told me that music played a great part in the life there. At this point Betty "chucked off" at me for being so serious. She became frankly bored.

Dorothy and Charlie both sang again, and Dr. G. and Betty exchanged jokes. Then Charlie sang again in a quite extraordinary way, and was praised by Dr. G., who was most enthusiastic over the quality of his voice. Clive Chapman played a march tune and Trevor played the cornet, but he soon forsook the tune of the piano and played over quite a large number of military bugle calls. This was one of the most impressive events of the sitting. He said that he had learnt to play since his death, and that it was much easier to learn on their side. As the piano continued to play the same tune Charlie sang again, but then something else occurred (and this is a note that Dr. G. wrote in my note-book at the time)—"March played. Voice singing notes not played on piano. An entirely independent melody."

Dr. G. also distinguished the sound of a banjo, and we all heard some whistling. The sitting ended at 11.30 p.m.

As before, my outstanding impression is that the evening seemed entirely natural. The conversation, which was similar to that of an ordinary evening (never, that is to say, reaching a high level) was free and unflagging. Charlie has a charming manner and voice. Betty gives one the impression of being a sweet child.

The patience of Clive Chapman and Miss Judd is remarkable. They seemed quite willing to let us (the visitors) have as much conversation as we possibly could, and assisted us in every possible way. There is still an enormous number of questions I want to ask, but this was a fascinating and instructive evening, in which perfect harmony prevailed.

THIRD SITTING

23/4/27-This was my third sitting at 9 Quarry Street. This time I was accompanied by Dr. G., Miss S. and J.B. The last two had not experienced this form of phenomenon before. Many of the happenings, methods, and talks were of the same nature as on the previous occasions. I give only a few of the events that stand out as unusual or novel in my opinion.

I heard very distinctly the sound of an instrument that certainly bore a strong resemblance to a violin. This continued for some time, and at one point was accompanied by whistling.

W., who was present for the first time, received a hearty welcome in Betty's best style. She said that she was glad that he had managed to have a free night at last and come along to make their acquaintance.

To him were addressed some very interesting remarks by "Nellie Dempster," whom he had known while she was on this side. She was the famous singer of the "Lonely Road" at the Dunedin Exhibition. Nellie, whom I had not previously met, sang this song, and to one who had heard it possibly scores of times before it certainly sounded very familiar.

The "Doe," as Betty calls him, asked Charlie to sing a song for him (hoping to hear the long sustained note at the end again) and handed to Clive a copy of "The Sands of the Desert," which was played. Charlie sang this, but in the midst of it Betty broke in—"That's not the one—what you wanted Doe, was 'Vale.'" This was very interesting, as at that very moment Dr. G. remembered that "Vale" was the song. The obvious surprise on the Doctor's face was a treat to watch.

I had asked our friends to bring along an acquaintance of mine. They assured me he was trying to speak, and later Betty said that he was playing an instrument—the violin's grandfather." She referred to a 'cello, the instrument that my friend played while on the earth. Clive did not realise just what was going on, and suggested that it was someone else who had previously played the 'cello for them, but Betty said that it was my friend-this spoken to me personally.

While Clive played the song "Always," several joined in at different times. Altogether all these took part—Betty, Charlie, Dorothy, a cornet, a violin, Jimmy, and Jim. One followed the other in, rapid succession.

I had a long connective conversation with Betty about several matters which I had previously enquired for—mostly concerning the conditions that obtained on the other side. Betty became quite serious, and spoke for quite half an hour without any difficulty with me. We carried on a rapid and interesting conversation—at least it was interesting to me! She said that people who passed away did not necessarily become fully conscious as soon as they reached the other side. Some were in a state that resembled sleep—everything was strange, they could not adjust themselves. Others who had a long illness which affected their spirits and mind, might have a long rest. Life was always changing-they had their duties to perform, and were under the control of what she called "Our Captain." This name she gave me after some hesitation and consultation with Charlie. Years and time did not count the same with them. She was a "wee tot" when she died, but now she was nine. They moved by thought—space made no difference. She could always speak to us as long as some music was played.

These, of course, are only short notes on an intensely interesting evening, which lasted for over three hours. They are supplementary to my other reports.

CHAPTER XII
Professional Magicians Find No Flaw

Mr. Chapman is always anxious to have any available professional or amateur—particularly professional "magicians," conjurers, etc., at his sittings, in order that his demonstrations might be closely scrutinised by experts in trickery. To this end he recently (on October 18th, 1927) invited one of the best known of these professionals, to wit, Carter the Great, to a sitting at his home. Mr. Carter gladly accepted the invitation and went out accompanied by a local gentleman, who is certainly one of the cleverest amateur conjurers in New Zealand. The sitting proved to be a good one, results well up to the average being achieved, and at its conclusion Mr. Carter expressed his astonishment and frankly admitted that he could not offer any explanation of the phenomena beyond what was claimed for it. He added that he thought he could reproduce all he had seen and heard in a manner sufficiently realistic for "show" purposes, but not without a great deal of intricate mechanism. "And," he said, "there are no signs of mechanism here of any kind." Asked what he thought of the "explanation" of ventriloquism, Mr. Carter answered promptly, "That is out of the question." The fact of the demonstration being carried out entirely in broad light made it all the more convincing. The local conjurer was even more astonished and just as satisfied that there was no trickery.

These testimonials, together with those of at least two practical ventriloquists and numerous ladies and gentlemen with long experience of the vaudeville stage, should surely outweigh the one or two confirmed sceptics who—after being present at one short sitting-could do no better in their anxiety to explain away the wonderful things they had heard than to maintain that Miss Judd was a ventriloquist capable of reproducing up to a dozen different voices and personalities without the slightest movement of mouth, lips, throat, or chest (one of these sceptics declared that "he noticed a strained look in Miss Judd's eyes when Charlie was sustaining a note for over twenty-four beats!") When it is remembered that most of these voices sing perhaps three or four different songs each; that the personality of the singer or speaker never varies, although the tone of voice (according to the nature of the conversation, and at times, to the nature of the instrument being played at the moment) frequently does; that answers are readily forthcoming to many questions that would require a wide general knowledge to supply; that two, and occasionally more, voices have been heard singing or speaking at the same time; that at every sitting some newcomer or curious unbeliever is constantly watching the medium and the investigator, who are in full view all the time; remembering all this, and more, anyone still adhering to the ventriloquist theory must also almost be prepared to declare Miss Judd to be the eighth wonder of the world.

Then there is the fact that on occasions no results have been got, despite the obvious anxiety of Mr. Chapman to bring the voices through. This, to the unbiassed mind, is a proof of genuineness rather than otherwise, because if the thing was a fraud, results would, for obvious reasons, be "manufactured" on each and every occasion. And once more it may be emphasised that, if this were fraud, the "performance" would undoubtedly be carried out in the dark, or in semi-darkness, the better to ensure safety from exposure. People have been led to expect "dark" seances, and fraudulent persons would certainly stick to this safety zone rather than risk disaster from too-keen eyes.

Many sitters, other than those quoted above, have written appreciative letters, but it has been impossible, or inconvenient, to obtain consent to publish the names of the writers; and to print a long series of these letters without the names appended would scarcely be convincing to those requiring proof.

CHAPTER XIII
Small, But Convincing Proofs

I myself have had but one really impressive experience away from the circles. This was quite recently—on November 2nd, 1927, at Mr. Thurston's home. Mr. Chapman and Miss Judd were about to begin a series of public demonstrations, and were leaving for Timaru at the end of the week. I half jocularly suggested to Betty that she might visit me at my home while Clive and Pearl were away. She answered "I'll try," and when I asked how I would know, she said "I'll give you a bump like I did before." This referred to a pronounced thud which was heard outside my house one evening when Mr. Chapman only was up there and the gramophone was playing. Betty had subsequently told us it was she. Well, on this occasion at Thurston's I thought no more of Betty's promise further than to wonder if in the course of a few days, say, she would knock me up. But that very night after reaching home I was sitting reading when I heard a thud as though someone had struck the outside wall with a heavy but muffled instrument such as a huge drumstick. I listened to see if I could hear any footsteps, but there were none (it was just midnight, and the wall is well away from the street and even from the neighbour's pathway), so I concluded that Betty had made good her promise with promptitude and despatch.

Soon afterwards I went to bed, but was awakened out of a deep sleep by some unknown agency, and a few moments afterwards there was the noise of a blow delivered apparently at the back of a chest of drawers which stood against the inside wall of my bedroom. I rose and looked at my watch; it showed exactly three o'clock. Lying awake, I heard just half an hour later a third thud, this time at the foot of my bed, over which I had thrown some surplus bedclothes. Nothing else happened that night, and I purposely refrained from telling Pearl (the medium) of the occurrence. At the next sitting, which happened to be the first Timaru sitting, Betty gleefully asked "Did you hear the knocks on the wall, Uncle George?" "Yes," I replied, "but you need not have wakened me up in the middle of the night." Whereupon she began to sing the song "Three O'clock in the Morning."

It was at the sitting at Thurston's already mentioned that an almost startling passage occurred. An elderly lady, Mrs. M, had been persuaded by her husband (who had been to several sittings) to attend for the first time. Mrs. M. was obviously a sceptic, and she sat silent and unbending throughout on the chair next mine. The sitting was nearing an end when she leaned towards her husband, who sat on her other hand, and whispered softly something which I did not catch. Immediately Charlie's voice rang out as though he were standing in the room.

"Don't go away with the wrong impression, Mrs. M," he said, "this is not ventriloquism."

And then he added in equally earnest tones, "Get that idea out of her head, won't you, Mr. M?" It was as though Charlie had pulled aside a curtain and thrust his head into the room to say the words. He had never in my experience spoken louder or more clearly, and I should say that it had been utterly impossible for the medium to have heard what Mrs. M. had said to her husband, and just as impossible for her to have spoken with such distinctness in a man's tones. It afterwards transpired that Mrs. M had whispered to her husband, "I think it is the young lady on the couch" (meaning the medium).

CHAPTER XIV
Extracts from Mr. Chapman's Diary

The following extracts from Mr. Chapman's diary are included with the intention of giving the reader some little idea of the varying experiences which the demonstrator, the medium, and their friends and visitors went through while this wonderful phase of communication was being developed. The diary is by no means a complete record, for, as Mr. Chapman remarks, it was extremely difficult for him to hear, and if he heard to remember, even a small part of all that happened at the sittings. Moreover, the diary was discontinued some months ago, when matters began to develop so quickly that little time was left, after Mr. Chapman's daily work was finished, for anything but the actual holding of sittings. Then, lately, came the preparations for the series of public demonstrations, which are being given as this book is in the press. The reader will, therefore, understand if these extracts should appear to him to be "scrappy," or hurriedly written.

28/2/1924. At lunch time a message came (through the table) very strongly and suddenly. HE CAME UNAWARES, it rapped; then OLGA PETROVA; then, very faintly, M.M. This last we could not understand until we found out by questioning that it stood for Martha Mansfield, the kinema star, who was burned fatally a little while ago. She made us understand that her photo was in the book that Pearl was reading at the time, and when we turned to the page upon which it appeared she gave a knock.

The same evening, about 9 o'clock, I was playing and singing at the piano. While singing "Beautiful Garden of Roses" I suddenly saw a brilliant white rose appear at the top left-hand corner of the page of music. It was a full-blown rose with an open centre, and it seemed to be on a dark background. At first I thought it must be my imagination, but Pearl also saw it: indeed, she described it to me first, and it was just as I had seen it. She said that her attention had been drawn to it by a beam of rosy light which led from the book she was reading to the rose on the music. I will never forget the sight; it was beautiful. Pearl says she saw a red rose in addition to the white one.

29/3/24. At tea time a message came through, strong but broken, F.R. (? FLOWING ROBES), then COUNCIL OF MARS. Next, in answer to the question as to who was the sender of this strange message, I AM ERIN; THEA. While this message was being spelled out I felt a sensation as of a strong electric current passing over my head at the end of each sentence. I had never felt this before, and it gives rise to the thought that possibly Mars could open up communication with this planet by means of electric or magnetic currents controlled by our spirit friends beyond. Why not?

2/4/24. After Mother had gone to bed, Dorothy came through and gave me a rare treat. She asked for "Sister," "Land of Long Ago," "The Long, Long Trail," and "Love Nest"; also two little trial pieces—"Sunset on the St. Lawrence" and "Perfect Day." The singing was beautiful, and the words quite plain. When "Sister" was being sung I could clearly hear an instrumental accompaniment: it sounded like a stringed instrument, the strings being "plucked." It may have been either a violin or a harp, but, whatever it was, the effect was exquisite, and the harmony perfect. In "The Long, Long Trail" I heard several voices singing at the same time—tenor, alto, soprano, etc. And the singers appeared to be so very happy.

17/4/24. Miss R (of Wellington), and Mr. G were round tonight, and Dorothy and Torrance gave them a great demonstration of singing. We could sometimes hear two voices, and now and again three, beautifully blended. In "Sister" we heard Torrance as we had never heard him before—every word was wonderfully distinct. Also, in "Land of Long Ago" we heard an instrument accompanying the singer, who sustained the notes, especially the last one, gloriously.

20/4/24. Pearl and I went to the Baptist Church again, and some of our friends from "the other side" came through and sang also. Both Pearl and I heard a lovely alto voice singing quite loudly; it seemed to be near the end of the seat in which we sat. During two or three of the hymns the seat in front of us moved gently to the time of the music.

8/5/24. At tea tonight the following names were spelt out: ALEC VON HERMOT, OTTO NAZIMOVA. Later in the evening a message came through saying that someone from the Royal Air Force would speak through Pearl later on.

10/5/24. While Pearl was sitting at the table—she was doing up her hair for the night—the letters T-R-A-V-E-R-S were spelled out. I asked who that was, and the answer came C-R-O-Y-D-O-N- A-E-R-OD-R-O-M-E. Following this came T-O-N-I-G-H-T-S P-A-P-E-R. So I asked should I look in the paper, and Y-E-S was spelled out. I looked through the newspaper, but could not locate the name, so I asked was it in the cables. N-0 was the answer. Again I searched the paper, and at last found the name Travers in an article entitled "Dropping to Death," which described briefly how young Travers was killed at the Croydon Aerodrome, London, over a month before. None of us had seen the article, and neither Pearl nor I had looked at the paper previously. Mother was in bed.

11/5/24. While I was playing the piano this evening the notes seemed to have quite a hollow sound (Mother noticed this also) and I felt a kind of throbbing through the music, like the distant beating of a motor, intermittent at first, but becoming more regular as I played. What it means or what it may develop into I do not yet know.

14/5/24. A long message was written through Pearl by Sahnaei this afternoon, explaining how those who are teachers (like himself) love to come and please and assist those who are helping us here on earth—meaning Dorothy and others on that sphere. 0h, if people would only wake up to the knowledge of the wonderful and beautiful thing that is at their very doors and try to understand the glory of what is beyond by the proofs that are given them. And it seems so wonderful that a child like Pearl should be chosen as an instrument to prove the life beyond, and that this instrument should be put in my care is thus a gift from God to me, and I would not exchange her for all the treasures of this world

16/5/24. At tea time Torrance, Martha Mansfield, and Dorothy came through. The following was spelled out: "Sarah St. Clair Gilmont. Massacred by Maoris."

25/5/24. This evening we heard whistling in harmony with the singing. Also, in several of the songs, we could hear different kinds of instruments being played; one in particular was really beautiful, the tone that of a pipe organ. It was one of the most enjoyable evenings we have had.

28/5/24. Mr. G called in again tonight, and we had more beautiful singing, even louder than on Sunday night. Dorothy came through Mr. G , and brought a lovely message to us, also a message of love and greeting from her father. I heard him singing while Dorothy was coming through. I easily recognised his voice, only, of course, it was purer, and had fewer limitations. But he cut off his notes in the old familiar way.

1/6/24. Mr. B called in this afternoon and told us he had heard faint singing in his home. This is, I expect, the result of his family having had Pearl so much in their company, thereby giving those on the other side a chance to transmit some power through Pearl to the B family. This is one way, I think, that the people will have the truth brought home to them, leaving them to themselves to develop the power which will enable our spirit friends to sing and speak to them more clearly,

3/6/24. Tonight we had two visitors, and heard three souls singing simultaneously in "Sweet and" Low." Instruments were also heard. At times the spirit voices joined in when Mr. G. was singing. Mr. P apparently did not get some of the singing, but this is only what I expected, as they give a new-comer only enough to convince him or to give him something to think over and create a desire for more.

10/6/24. Tonight we all went to Reynolds', as arranged by Dorothy and others. At first the voices were very faint, but as the sitting proceeded most of the persons present heard our spirit friends quite clearly; some also heard instruments, one a violin, one a flute, one a clarinet, and one an organ. I consider that the results were very good, considering that the room was a strange one and that most of the sitters were new to the whole thing.

11/6/24. Tonight Martha sang so loudly and clearly that I felt that I need only turn round to see her standing near me. Her voice simply filled the room; it was the loudest I have yet heard. I do believe that our dear spirit friends could come right out whenever they chose, but will not give more at a time than is necessary for their purpose. It would scarcely do for most people to hear the voices as I have heard them some-times; it is better that they should be brought to realise gradu-ally and, as it were, earn their reward.

15/6/24. At lunch time, as we sat quietly eating our lunch a name was spelled out through the table ALLAN LOCK-HART. We knew him in earth life (he has been over about four years), but had not given him I thought for perhaps two or three years. I myself did not know he was on the other side until his name came through today. After this something else was spelled out, but I cannot recall it, except that they told us it was from "Cyrus" a personality of long ago.

17/6/24. At a sitting this evening three of us—Mr. R , Robin and I—, sang as loudly as we could in "Sister," yet Torrance's tenor voice was heard above us all. Again, Mr. R sang "Love's Old Sweet Song," and Martha harmonised most beautifully with him. It was all wonderful. Then in "The Sheik" two voices were heard, a man's and a woman's, and the high sustained notes were wonderful, especially the woman's. After the song was finished Mrs. R happened to remark that the woman's power appeared to be used up, whereupon our spirit friends demanded the last verse and chorus over again, and sang them louder than ever, finishing with a tremendous volume of sound. After the singing we had a demonstration of power with the table, all of us standing round it. The power produced made it impossible for Robin to raise the table from the floor; and he stood at the opposite end to Pearl ! Following this we had a further demonstration, this time with the piano. This was in the dark, but it was wonderful all the same. The instrument rocked about, and our spirit friends played all sorts of music—some of it very beautiful—upon it. We also heard one voice (Torrance's, I think) singing to this music.

21/6/24. At tea time we were talking about Miss Christie, a well-known member of the Theosophical Society, when the table moved as though shaken with laughter, and then spelled out, "I am she," adding that she had found things over there to be quite different to what she had thought when on earth.

24/6/24. After tea three visitors came to an arranged sitting, but did not get as much as they might, for, as it turned out, our spirit friends knew as soon as the visitors arrived that they had come merely to get "proofs." If they had come with faith in the world beyond they would have got more. It was the old story of the Pharisees who "wanted a sign." Later in the evening we had the piano playing in the dark, and the name PETER was spelled out by striking notes on the piano. After this our spirit friends gave a demonstration with the table, pressing it down so that each of us had to exert our strength to the utmost in order to lift it.

So that these visitors tonight were very fortunate to get as much as they did, seeing that they came in a criticising mood.

27/6/24. At the sitting tonight Charlie sang louder than I had ever heard him : he could be heard above Mrs. B 's voice and Horace's cornet together. Then came another discovery. I played a song called "Wodonga" several times over, and Charlie could be heard calling out "Emmie, Emmie," to Mrs. B , who is his sister. At first she did not understand, not until I told her to speak to him, which she did, and he told her to "bring Laura next week."

During the evening Mr. B played his ukulele while I played the piano, and I noticed that a sustained droning note was the result, and that our spirit friends were able to speak on this while Pearl was in the room. This is worth developing; it may open up great possibilities.

2/7/24. Tonight Charlie soon opened up a conversation with his sister, Mrs. B., and I could hear him quite clearly answer her questions. It was wonderful to listen to someone who had been out of this world for years talking to his sister who is still on earth. The day of speaking mediums is, so far as I can see, nearly ended; this phase brings our spirit-friends right to us, direct, in every way.

14/7/24. We were at Reynolds' tonight, and, after supper, everyone except Pearl and I were told to take up positions in different parts of the house while I played "Home, Sweet Home." They did so, and on their return each one declared that he or she had heard beautiful instruments (all different) accompanying the music.

7/8/24. At lunch today ROSINA was spelled out on the table, and we tried to guess who it was.

Then came the message "Surely you have not forgotten me so soon" to Pearl, who then remembered that Martha Mansfield had taken the part of Rosina in a recent picture.

15/8/24. The name JOBE was spelled out at the table this evening, and it turned out to be Granddad's brother. (I found out afterwards that that was the way he always mis-spelled his name).

19/8/24. After tea tonight we went to Reynolds' to our private circle. The singing was beautiful, and I could hear dear Dorothy's voice quite close to me, and while she sang "Garden of Roses" I could distinctly discern the scent of roses all round me. All the singing was good, and in "Home, Sweet Home" the instrumental accompaniment was glorious; it sounded like a full orchestra at times, only more heavenly.

23/8/24. Part of tonight was very merry, our spirit friends being particularly happy. Charlie made us laugh so much that he himself had to join in it—a good hearty laugh that was wonderful to hear. Also we could hear Torrance laughing. I am afraid this would shock some of our unco' serious orthodox church friends. At the end of this happy sitting our spirit friends kept us still and quiet for about five minutes. We seemed to be surrounded by an exquisite heavenly peace; it was wonderful.

27/8/24. This was Mother's birthday, and at the tea table the following came through and wished her Many Happy Returns of the Day:—Dorothy, Martha, Emily (Granny), Emily Kaye, Torrance, Jack Sutherland, Jack Watts, Kitchener, Sahnaei, Charlie, Horace, Arty, Nurse Cavell, Nurse Eunice, Granddad, and several others. Violet (my sister) was with us at the table, and her husband and a visitor called in after tea.

Then our spirit friends gave us a splendid entertainment. It was a sort of spiritual birthday party in honour of Mother, and it made her very happy.

3/9/24. At the sitting tonight Torrance asked one of the visitors, Mrs. C_, to go out into the hall and shut the door, assuring her that she would from there still be able to hear him sing. "Sister" was the song, and Mrs. C declared that she heard Charlie's voice distinctly above my voice and the sound of the piano. Violet also had the same experience. Both of them heard the instruments as well as the voices in "Salopia" while out in the hall.

14/9/24. At the sitting tonight a new voice came through, a voice such as we had never heard before. It was quite loud, but indescribably glorious; I deemed it to come from one of the higher spheres, it was so pure.

22/9/'24. About 9 p.m. I was playing the piano when Charlie came and had a talk with me, and also sang. His singing and speaking voice were both louder than I had heard from him before, and he was in a merry and happy mood. I did enjoy his company, and the visit was a very pleasant surprise. And all this went on while Pearl was at the table reading.

29/9/24. Tonight we held a sitting for Miss B. R.'s benefit, and had great results. While Betty was in the front room getting her music, and I was playing the piano, Charlie called out "Betty" as loudly as I could have done, and she heard him in the other room.

6/10/24. At the sitting tonight our friends spoke on the sound of chords only.

7/10/24. At R.'s tonight I did not hear things as clearly as I have done on other nights, but I was not feeling very well, which may account for it. We tried the chords again, and I heard Dorothy and Charlie calling out.

8/10/24. Several messages came through the table at tea time tonight, amongst them was spelled out "Ruby Diamond; Poisoned." It seems that, when conditions are good, our spirit friends bring some other spirit along to spell out its name, and perhaps particulars concerning itself.

28/11/24. At the sitting tonight, old Mrs._ , who is very deaf, heard our spirit friends very plainly talking and singing. I find it difficult to describe adequately the things that happen at our sittings; there has been such a wonderful development in the talking phase, it would need a reporter to take down all the conversation. I have just to do my best to give a general idea of the proceedings.

30/12/24. We had no sooner got settled down tonight at the tea-table than Charlie came and spelled out "Listen." Then came the following, faintly:—"Widow Ete, Lorraine. " I asked who it was, and Charlie answered "Look in today's Times." As we had not the Times in the house, Pearl went, after tea, to her mother's and got it, and there, sure enough, in the cables, was a reference to the death of a Widow Ete, of Lorraine. The cable added that the woman had had a premonition of her death. This seems to me to be a wonderful proof of life beyond, and shows that some souls that are good can come to us quite soon after passing over.

28/3/25. The sitting tonight was at Mr. R 's. Wee Betty had a long talk to him about her "school' life" over there; telling him of their lessons and their teachers—who are wonderfully kind and loving.

4/4/25. Sitting at Mr. R 's tonight, with fine results. Mrs. K had a chat with her daughter, who went over when about eight years old. Mrs. K easily recognised the voice of her daughter, who asked to be remembered to two of her brothers. Now, no one in the room knew of these two boys except the mother and Mr. R., and neither mentioned the names until they had been mentioned by the little one "over there." Wee Betty had a further talk with Mr. R about her schooling. They are shown, said Betty, by means of pictures, how flowers are made, for instance, and many other interesting things. Boys and girls assemble together, and the teachers are of the same (earthly) nationality as the children they are teaching. When these children wish to converse and do not know each other's language they use the universal thought language.

18/8/25. Wee Betty told us tonight that the trees over there have beautifully coloured leaves and flowers, all in harmony, not gaudy; and that the birds were beautifully coloured too. Also that they had roads there which were smooth and even, and each a distinct colour. "There are no fences around the houses," added Betty, "just very low hedges of beautiful shrubs which anyone could step over."

20/8/25. After Wee Betty had talked to us tonight, all sorts of strange sounds were heard from the other side, as if they were preparing for something. They had told us there was a big surprise in store for us, so we are wondering what it will be.

22/8/25. Just after tea I was playing the "Colonel Bogey" march, and Pearl was cleaning her boots, when we both heard quite clearly over our heads some instrument playing the march in the bass solo. It appeared to be a wind instrument, something like a magnified flute of exquisite tone. The sound came and went in waves, and I could hear it echoing far above me.

27/9/25. Last night I dreamed, or seemed to dream, that I was looking out over a stormy sea, where a fierce blizzard was raging. It was a big bay I was looking across, and I could see the foam topped waves driven by the wind. On the left, about half a mile away, was a rocky island with steep cliffs. On the less steep side, and near the foot of the cliff, was a large ship at anchor. She was fitted up with a big wireless aerial, the masts being latticed and very high. I could distinctly see the snow on the face of the rocky island, which stood about 800 ft. out of the water; the snow was also being driven into the rigging and recesses of the vessel at anchor. Out in the bay I could just discern two other vessels fighting their way through the blizzard. One was small, like a tug, and the other, a large one, was further away and scarcely visible through the driving snow.

On the summit of the island was a large wireless station, the masts of which were built of lattice work, just as those of the vessel beneath were. And I seemed to hear someone speaking and saying that they had established communication with all parts of the world.

Now, what does all this mean? For it seemed to me to be more than a mere dream; rather a vision. Perhaps it may mean that those on the other side have been able to link up with our wireless stations and that before long, the world will get some startling messages through. There seems to me to be nothing to stop them sending through electric wireless, seeing that electricity is easy to handle, so far as they are concerned. The storm may represent the stress and turmoil the whole world is going through, while the struggling ships may mean that we here must face the storm that is raging, and that out of the storm will come true faith and revelation and messages from beyond. The world at present is like the storm I saw—cold, driving, blinding, and confusing; the rocky island represents the truth which nothing can shake, and the wireless station on the island those souls which are tuned in to the faith receiving and sending out messages of hope. The ships were heading for the island of truth, so I look upon this dream, or vision, as an encouragement to face the storm fearlessly. The words I heard must mean that communication has been established by the faith of those who believe, and that very soon now direct communication will be opened up, most likely through our wireless machines.

8/5/26. At Mr. R 's tonight, and one of the most beautiful evenings we have had. Charlie sang splendidly with Dorothy in "Vale," and then, as I played some chords on the organ, he sustained a note for upwards of five minutes; it was simply startling, and we thought he was never going to stop. At the same time other sounds gradually came in, and at one time I heard what appeared to be two trumpets playing together and harmonising beautifully. Once we all listened to a conversation between Wee Betty and Hunter: their words could be heard quite clearly, and when Mr. R mentioned that he could hear, Wee Betty turned on him like a flash and told him that it was rude of him to listen to a private conversation.

19/5/26. After tea I played the piano for about two hours. After I had stopped both Mother and I could distinctly hear the murmur of several voices talking. I went outside (both back and front doors) to see if anyone was about, but everything was perfectly still. When I came in I could again hear the voices, and Mother said she could still hear the talking going on. It was the sound of women's and men's voices in conversation, as though through a fog, so I put it down to those beyond. It is possible that they may have stored a good bit of power from the sound and vibrations of the piano, and then let us hear them talking. We could not catch any of the words, just the tone of the voices, of which there seemed to be several.

22/5/26. At Mr. R_'s, Mrs. K_'s little daughter Joy came several times tonight, and chatted with her mother. It was beautiful to hear the affectionate conversation between them, and the child's voice was so distinct. I could hear almost every word, although at the organ, and so in the midst of the greatest noise. One of the sitters was a confessed atheist, and Wee Betty took him to task, telling him he was a mere child in the understanding of life. He asked her all sorts of questions, and she quite held her own in her replies. It was a good sitting, in spite of the sceptic's presence.

25/5/26. At a sitting at R_'s tonight our friends directed us to sit at certain places round the table, with Mrs. B and Robin on it. Our friends then demonstrated their power by taking charge of the table, pressing it down with a terrific pressure, shifting the weight from one to another of us, and moving the table round the room in a most amusing fashion, and forcing each of us into our respective chairs.

9/6/26. I was in bed today with a bad cold, and during the night was awakened by Dorothy's voice singing Tennyson's beautiful "Song of Sleep." And —I could scarce believe my senses—there she stood' beside my bed, smoothing my hair, and, oh, so gently adjusting the blankets around me. I could feel her dear hands on my head, and as I was about to speak to her as she finished the song, she drew slowly away and vanished before my eyes. I could see her hand as she withdrew it from my head; she was solid and real, just as any mortal would be.

I will never forget the experience or the wonderful happiness it brought me. The song I had not heard for two years, but it is one which holds for me very tender memories.

19/8/26. A sitting in the Blue Room. All the voices particularly clear, especially Wee Betty, who at times seemed to be right out in the room. Torrance came and sang just in the way he used to in Mills Street. Mrs. D 's (one of the sitters) aunt also came and sang and spoke to her. We could hear Charlie helping her here and there. A Zulu chief spoke to us, too, but in his native tongue; it was extremely funny to hear Betty interpreting according to how it sounded to her. Suddenly, in the middle of the sitting Charlie asked us to keep silent for a little while; then he said, "Play 'Sad Little Eyes' for Nellie Dempster." While I was playing it we could hear Charlie instructing her how to use the power and to control the sound waves so as to make her voice heard. At first she broke, and we heard Charlie again instructing her, the words "See, like this," coming through distinctly. Soon she managed to get through, but faintly; then, as she gradually got control, her voice became louder and clearer. She had not the power to speak this time, but no doubt she will soon. Charlie asked me to get "The Lonely Road" for her. This soul used to sing at the Exhibition; she passed over only a few weeks ago.

24/8/26. A sitting at Mr. R_'s. Peter was well to the fore tonight; he had a long chat with Mr. R, describing the way in which they help the souls of the coloured people over there.

Nellie came again, and sang "Sad Little Eyes." Her voice sounded just as it used to in the Australian court at the Exhibition. She managed to speak a few words, saying it was wonderful to be able to come and sing to us like this. She seems to have a lovely nature.

9/9/26. We held a special sitting at home tonight in accordance with a request by Dorothy a couple of nights ago. Only Mother, Pearl, and I were present, and it was one of the very best sittings to date. Conditions were good, we were all happy and cheery, and our friends beyond seemed to experience no difficulty in making themselves easily heard, both in singing and speaking. I suppose they just love to get the chance to come to us here on earth under favourable conditions, for then they are able to bring themselves, spiritual body and all, quite close to us. When we on our part are able to shut out all gloom, doubt, worry, business affairs, etc., and receive our friends with open arms and full of joy, then we get everything from them short of actually seeing them. I do not remember a sitting at which so many came through so loudly and clearly. They all seemed so full of life and bubbling over with joyfulness. Dorothy's voice was identically the same as her earth voice used to be. While the various souls were speaking I could hear another voice (a woman's) singing the song that was being played; a voice which became clearer and clearer as time went on. When I broke into "Horsey, Keep Your Tail Up" Betty sang it, but introduced words of her own which were a hit at Pearl, who had had her hair bobbed. It was a splendid evening altogether.

26/9/26. As I lay in bed thinking, and was just about to blow out the light, I heard a child's voice (which I at once recognised as Wee Betty's) right close to my ear. It was low but distinct, and said "I's here, Uncle Clive," in a plaintive tone. I was delighted to hear the little soul's voice so direct (and when I was alone, too), and said something in reply. She then became excited, and said "Oo, look, look; See, Ooo," as though some extraordinary thing had come into her sight. Then I just glimpsed a form shaped like a large and elongated Rugby football, or a small Zeppelin, about six feet in length. It was dark brown with a faint beautiful blue band across the middle (lengthways). It remained visible only two or three seconds. These experiences give me great comfort, and I set them down here to show what can be given to those of us who really believe and trust, not in the "easy" way but by facing everything for it. That is the only way to help those dear ones to come close to us individually.

5/10/26. At R's tonight rather a remarkable thing took place. Robin was (at Betty's request) turning on the wireless and now and then giving lots of volume, while in between these wireless items, I played the piano. Once we heard Betty's voice right in the loud speaker horn. That was good, but a little later, while the wireless was silent and I had ceased playing the piano, we all heard a voice speaking in a whisper and sounding as though half way between Robin and Pearl (who were seven feet or so apart). "Yes, that would be nice, wouldn't it?" said the voice, as though in answer to a remark which Robin had just made. The room is a large one, and I was at the opposite end, but I heard the whispered words distinctly.

It looks as though our dear ones are seizing every opportunity to get further through to us. This will probably lead to hearing them occasionally between the musical items. I mean to investigate and follow up the idea.

12/10/26. At Mr. G,'s studio tonight. The piano was a good one for sound-waves. Some pianos, by the way, are better than others for this purpose, and I feel very quickly the effect of what the other side do with the instrument. Occasionally a distinct buzzing vibration, almost electrical, can be felt through the keys, sometimes just here and there, and sometimes not at all. Occasionally a kind of current runs through my fingers. Again a key here and there feels as though it was on a cushion, or so sensitive that it goes down almost before I touch it. When Mr. G. asked Betty tonight if she would not like to be back on earth again, she answered most emphatically, "Not on your life : it's too nice over here." "But," she added, "we love to come in this way to help the people to understand the real truth." It must certainly be a great adventure for those souls to come so near the earth in so natural a manner. It must be borne in mind that there are many spheres between those dear ones in the brighter spheres and this world, and the difficulties they encounter may be dimly understood when we remember they have to journey through these intermediate spheres (with their abundant and varying conditions) in order to get to us, and even then take the chance of our being able to make the conditions on this side such that it will be possible for them to stay a while with us.

20/10/26. We went to Mr. G's studio for a circle tonight, but for a long time the voices were very faint, and our friends seemed to have difficulty in getting through. There was a dance going on in the room below, and I thought that this perhaps was the disturbing element, but on my asking Wee Betty she said, very faintly, "No." I questioned some of the others, and Dorothy and Betty particularly appeared to be very much upset about something. Mr. G, I had noticed, was not very bright tonight, and Mother seemed a little moody, so I was at a loss what to do; everything seemed upset. Something was obviously wrong, and when Charlie was able to come through he said we had no idea how difficult it was for them to get through sometimes. Then I did my best to cheer things up; I got Mr. G and Mother to talk to Wee Betty, and soon that dear little soul began to chat away in her old bright way. Then things improved, and I was glad, after the un-promising beginning. But it made me sad to hear Dorothy and Betty so upset. All this goes to show how necessary it is for every one in the circle to be really bright and happy, and so help our dear ones to come through easily. They themselves are naturally bright and happy and try hard to bring that con-dition into the circle. Even one person gloomy, or otherwise than bright, has an effect upon them. When everyone is in harmony they come through easily.

31/10/26. During a long sitting at R 's tonight Nellie came through and sang very clearly "Sad Little Eyes." Strange to say two of the persons in the room could not hear a note of this song. Sometimes this sort of thing happens, no matter how good the conditions, which shows that those on the other side are able to prevent, if they choose, some persons from hearing what all the rest in the room can hear plainly. On occasions I have been unable to hear what everyone else was hearing; and again, I have heard things that nobody else got, in spite of my close proximity to the piano or organ. Once tonight I played "Sympathy," and Dorothy started to sing the verse, then Wee Betty joined in, and finally Charlie, so that we had three voices singing together in the chorus : the harmony was very beautiful. Other wonderful singing was heard this night. After the sitting, Pearl and most of the others, moved to the fireside. I kept on at the organ, and pulling out some stops, played over some hymns with the full power of the instrument. Presently, to everyone's surprise, a beautiful voice could be heard singing at the other side of the room to that on which we were sitting. We all heard it, and the louder I played, the louder sang the voice. Then other voices joined in. It was a revelation.

31/10/26. Tonight we had an arranged sitting at Lady le Fleming's. Among the sitters were Mr. and Mrs. Slater (vaudeville artists), who have traveled all round the world, and who told me afterwards that they had never witnessed such convincing results from attempts to communicate with the beyond as this phase of mediumship had brought. He very kindly gave me permission to use his or his wife's name in support of this statement. If everyone would receive those dear souls as he does great results would always follow. Several of the band sang tonight, Nellie giving "Sad Little Eyes," and some of her notes seemed to fill the room. "Love's Old Sweet Song" was sung beautifully by Martha. She appeared diffident about singing this, possibly because she had already sung tonight, and we could plainly hear Wee Betty urging her to come forward. We all sang the chorus, and the harmonising between Martha and Jim was glorious. Grace came along and sang, and though, as Charlie told us, she was far away, we could hear her distinctly.

3/11/26. A sitting in "The Blue Room" tonight. Mr. G here. Betty gave him a great time, being in her brightest mood. Once she said something about smoking injuring him, remarking that he "was trying to get through a hole in the fence"; meaning, I suppose, that he was not taking proper care of himself and might come over too soon. Again, she said, when he referred to his body, "Oh, we don't want that here, we want your spook." She then sang "Barney Google," and played her usual trick on me by racing at a terrific bat over the last line or two. No matter how fast I play she always easily beats me to the finish, yet enunciates every word. This is still another poser for those sceptics who endeavour to explain away the voices with the one word "Ventriloquism." Another poser was when Betty one night went through with that tongue-twisting rigmarole "Peter Piper picked a peck of pickled pepper," etc., it being well known that ventriloquists never speak the letter P.

6/11/26. Tonight while two voices were harmonising in "Life's Dream is O'er" we distinctly heard two others—Betty and Peter it was—talking to each other.

10/11/26. We held a sitting in "The Blue Room" this afternoon, of course in full daylight. While Martha was singing
her favourite "Love's Old Sweet Song," two other voices sang
with her, one—a baritone—sounding very close to me at the
piano. This voice took me by surprise, it was so loud and close
to me, and such a rich, deep baritone. I have never heard a
voice sing so loudly since I began this work. Possibly the fact
that we were all singing (it was in the chorus where we all
joined in) which created greater sound vibrations for them to
operate upon.

22/11/26. Today Mr. and Mrs. Sh_ visited us, and during the
evening I tried the latter with the glass and board. She turned
out to be a splendid medium for this phase of the power. First
of all Dorothy's name was spelled out, and she conversed with
me in the same old way that she used to do through Pearl.
She spelled out "Do let C (Mrs S.) try alone," so I took my
hand off the glass, which then spelled out "Dear old boy." I
thought this referred to me, but no, for next came "No hair,"
which could refer only to Mr. Mac_, who was also present.
The sender of the message turned out to be Wee Betty. Mr.
Mac's Christian name was mentioned, though none of us had
known what it was, and messages of a semi-private and comforting nature came to him.

8/12/26. This afternoon Mr. and Mrs. Sh_ n (who are vaudeville artists) and two others in the same profession (Mr. and
Mrs. H) called to see us, and we soon adjourned to "The Blue
Room." I asked Dorothy to let me know through C's hand if
we could get the voices. After a rather long wait a message

came saying "Zara says 'Welcome to you all.'" Then came "Bless you all; try; Dorothy," and the handwriting in this message was identical with that in Dorothy's messages which come through Pearl. Faint voices came after this, and then a small table upon which C's hands were resting began to move, first gently and then violently. Would Dorothy give one knock if she was there, I asked, and immediately C jumped out of her chair; somebody, she said, had pinched her leg once. This was the reply, given thus instead of by a knock. The table next moved towards each of us in turn (C still keeping contact), and when I played a hymn beautiful voices joined in. C was a little bit afraid at first, but she will soon get used to it, and good results should come through her.

2/2/27. Today we held a sitting in The Blue Room (in broad daylight) with very beautiful results. Wee Betty come very close to us. She had become very much attached to Mr. 0, who is leaving Dunedin on Monday, and it was quite affecting to hear her speaking to him today. Anyone hearing this sensitive little soul, her heart obviously full of pure love for this earth friend of hers, could not but believe in the reality of the life beyond. They are far more sensitive to the higher emotions than we are, and glory in bringing love and happiness to us here.

12/2/27. We held a sitting at K 's tonight. Our dear ones seemed to be very busy in many ways. First they asked us to wait a while before starting off with the music. In the meantime Pearl, while under control, drew several sketches.

One was of a ship, underneath which was written; "Every ship will find a harbour"; another of a star within a heart, and beneath it "Star of hope and love." Also a message reading "The road may be narrow and rough, but it is worth while." Next a message came to the effect that we were to sit still for ten minutes and if we saw or heard anything to say so. But while we were waiting quietly a knock came at the front door, and we had to answer it, which spoiled the whole thing. More sketches came, with explanations by a new control who was apparently a clever scientific engineer; sketches of a balloon, an airship of strange design, and a huge aeroplane. The writing was quite different to any other that had come through Pearl. The voices came later, but were not so loud as usual, but at times two or more could be heard harmonising.

14/2/27. A sitting that was in many ways remarkable was held at K's tonight. The singing was splendid; Nellie, Dorothy, and Martha being specially distinct. Wee Betty, as usual, had us all laughing, while Peter came out very strongly. During the evening we were asked to have a demonstration of the piano phenomena in the dark, and the results were truly startling. One soul came and played a song which Mr. K recognised as a favourite of his sister's. He alone knew this, and it was she who was playing it. Then came a scout drum-march, tapped out on the piano, the performer also playing an air quite unknown to Pearl or to me. When he gave his name it was Cecil Mason, who was known to the Ks. Next came an old friend of mine, one Arthur Pitts, who played the "Destiny" valse, which, I remembered, he had been fond of playing on his violin. Others also came and played.

Then, in the full light, we heard sounds which appeared to reach far out into space, and other sounds akin to many machines being worked. Sahnaei came and, on "Arabia," almost took control of Pearl in trance. We could hear him talking to her, and several others also spoke to her.

At what may be termed a "casual" sitting at Mrs._'s (Timaru) on November 13th, 1927, some rather remarkable features were noticed. 'Wee Betty was again the chief spokeswoman and was in her best form. Several of those present had never previously been to a sitting. Among them were a young married couple, friends of the hostess. The latter began by putting Betty through an examination, so to speak, asking her to name in turn the strangers present. Betty did so, even to the nondescript dog "Micky," who was ensconced on the sofa, and when she came to the young husband referred to she promptly named him "Smiler." This evidently astonished his wife—as well as confusing the husband—and she remarked that this nick-name was rarely used outside the home because she objected to it. No one in "The Blue room" party could possibly have known that this gentleman was called "Smiler" in his own home. Next Betty remarked "Mrs. Reynolds" (a Dunedin lady) "is here too," "Oh, no, dear," said the hostess, "Mrs. Reynolds is not here tonight." "Yes she is," asserted Betty, and on being asked where, answered : " On the mantelpiece." There, sure enough, was a photo of the Dunedin lady, also photos of others whom Betty duly named, all except one, which turned out to be one of the hostess's mother in her wedding gown., "Micky's picture is there too," said Betty.

This was denied, but it was found that Betty was referring to a calendar which hung upon the wall and upon which was drawn or painted a picture of a dog. Again, this young soul, when asked the hostess's maiden name, answered "You're a flower." "Yes, dear, but what flower?" said Mrs. . "Not Buttercup," said Betty. "No, not Buttercup, dear." Then the young voice began to sing the song "Buttercups and Daisies," and Mrs. admitted that her name was Daisy. On this evening Charlie, Nellie, Dorothy, and others sang and spoke a few words to us, but it was largely a "Wee Betty" night, the child soul demonstrating in most convincing fashion her quickness of wit as well as her sweetness of character.

END